QUIPS

QUOTES

ZINGERS

&

ONE LINERS

....WITH A LITTLE PHILOSOPHY,

A LITTLE REALITY,

SOME JOKES &

USELESS

INFORMATION

As compiled by Joe Blatnick
Illustrations by Jose Bigith

PREFACE

Over a great many years, I wrote down most of the funny signs which I saw, jotted down the odd joke or two, made note of philosophical statements and just generally zeroed in on things of interest. Once the internet became the endless source that it is, the binders truly began piling up. As my family and friends began questioning my purpose in assembling such a collection, I told them that one day they would appear in a book. Well, here it is! However, I've just been the catalyst. Although some of the content is original, most is the brilliant work of others. Unfortunately, I know not who they are, but I owe them many thanks. Read on and enjoy.

SOMETHING ELSE

Some items appear in more than one section of the book. This was done deliberately because that particular item is also applicable elsewhere.

TABLE OF CONTENTS

Advice	1	Life	153
Age	5	Marriage	165
Ambiguity	9	Medical	169
Aphorisms	17	Moral of the Story	175
Animals	21	Old Age	179
The Better Half	25	Oxymorons	203
Blondes	31	Panic	207
The Boss	45	Philosophical	211
Bumper Stickers	49	Point Of View	225
Bureaucracy	53	Politicians	231
Church	57	Ponderisms	235
Economics	61	Psychiatrists	239
Ethnic Humour	65	Puns	243
The Fairer Sex	77	Putdowns	251
Family Pets	83	Quotes	257
For Men Only	89	Raising Children	277
Friends	93	Reality	291
Government	97	Rednecks	307
Helpful	103	Retirement	311
Husband & Wife	111	Self Depreciation	319
Illusions	123	Sex	323
Insults	127	Signs	327
Junk Mail	131	So What Else Is New	333
Language	135	Sports	339
A Legend	149	Words	351

ADVICE

OLD FARMER'S ADVICE

Your fences need to be horse-high and pig-tight.

Keep skunks and bankers at a distance.

Life is simpler when you plow around the stumps.

A bumble bee is considerably faster than a tractor.

Words that soak into your ears are whispered not yelled.

Meanness don't just happen overnight.

Forgive your enemies; it messes up their heads.

Do not corner something that you know is not you.

It don't take a very big person to carry a grudge.

You cannot unsay a cruel word.

Every path has a few puddles.

When you wallow with pigs, expect to get dirty.

The best sermons are lived, not preached.

Most of the stuff people worry about, ain't never gonna happen anyway.

Don't judge folks by their relatives.

Remember that silence is sometimes the best answer.

Live a good and honorable life, then when you get older and think back, you'll enjoy it a second time.

Don't interfere with somethin' that ain't bothering you none.

Timing has a lot to do with the outcome of a rain dance.

Sometimes you get, and sometimes you get got.

The biggest troublemaker you'll probably ever have to deal with, watches you form the mirror every mornin'. This is probably ALL so TRUE!

If you get to thinkin' you're a person of some influence, try orderin' somebody else's dog around.

Live simply, love generously, care deeply, speak kindly, and leave the rest to God.

Don't pick a fight with an old man. If he is too old to fight, he'll just kill you.

AGE

WILL ROGER'S'
ABOUT GROWING OLDER...

First: Eventually you will reach a point when you stop lying about your age and start bragging about it.

Second: The older we get, the fewer things seem worth waiting in line for.

Third: Some people try to turn back their odometers. Not me. I want to know why I look this way. I've traveled a long way, and some of the roads weren't paved.

Fourth: When you are dissatisfied and would like to go back to your youth, think of Algebra.

Fifth: You know you are getting old when everything either dries up or leaks.

Sixth: I don't know how I got over the hill without getting to the top.

Seventh: One of the many things no one tells you about aging is that it's such a nice change from being young.

Eighth: One must wait until evening to see how splendid the day has been.

Ninth: Being young is beautiful, but being old is comfortable and relaxed.

Tenth: Long ago, when men cursed and beat the ground with sticks, it was called witchcraft. Today it's called golf.

And Finally: If you don't learn to laugh at trouble, you won't have anything to laugh at when you're old.

AMBIGUITY

QUESTIONS THAT HAUNT ME!

How important does a person have to be before they are considered assassinated instead of just murdered?

Once you're in heaven, do you get stuck wearing the clothes you were buried in for eternity?

Why does a round pizza come in a square box?

What disease did cured ham actually have?

How is it that we put man on the moon before we figured out it would be a good idea to put wheels on luggage?

Why is it that people say they 'slept like a baby' when babies wake up every few hours?

Why are you IN a movie, but you're ON television?

Why do people pay to go up tall buildings and then put money in binoculars to look at things on the ground?

Why do doctors leave the room while you change? They're going to see you naked anyway...

Why is 'bra' singular and 'panties' plural?

Why do toasters always have a setting that burns the toast to a horrible crisp, which no decent human being would eat?

If Jimmy cracks corn and no one cares, why is there a stupid song about him?

Why does Goofy stand erect while Pluto remains on all fours? They're both dogs!

If corn oil is made from corn and vegetable oil is made from vegetables, what is baby oil made from?

Do the Alphabet song and Twinkle, Twinkle Little Star have the same tune?

Quips, Quotes, Zingers & One Liners

Why did you just try singing the two songs above?

Did you ever notice that when you blow in a dog's face, he gets mad at you, but when you take him for a car ride, he sticks his head out the window?

Why, why, why do we press harder on a remote control when we know the batteries are getting weak?

Why do banks charge a fee on 'insufficient funds' when they know there is not enough money?

Why does someone believe you when you say there are four billion stars, but check when you say the paint is wet?

Why do they use sterilized needles for death by lethal injection?

Why doesn't Tarzan have a beard?

Why does Superman stop bullets with his chest, but ducks when you throw a revolver at him?

Why do Kamikaze pilots wear helmets?

Why is it that no matter what color bubble bath you use, the bubbles are always white?

Is there ever a day that mattresses are not on sale?

Why do people constantly return to the refrigerator with hopes that something new to eat will have materialized?

Why do people keep running over a thread a dozen times with their vacuum cleaner, then reach down, pick it up, examine it, then put it down to give the vacuum one more chance?

Why is it that no plastic bag will open from the end you first try?

How do those dead bugs get into those enclosed light fixtures?

Why is it that whenever you attempt to catch something that's fallen off the table you always manage to knock something else over?

In winter why do we try to keep the house as warm as it was in the summer when we complained about the heat?

How come you never hear father-in-law jokes?

And my favorite...

One out of four people is mentally ill. If all three of your best friends are okay, does that mean it's you?

~~~

THE PHILOSOPHY OF AMBIGUITY:
FOR THOSE WHO LOVE THE PHILOSOPHY OF AMBIGUITY, AS WELL AS THE IDIOSYNCRASIES OF ENGLISH

Please enjoy and understand the following:

1) Don't sweat the petty things and don't pet the sweaty things.

2) One tequila, two tequila, three tequila, floor.

3) Atheism is a non-prophet organization.

4) If man evolved from monkeys and apes, why do we still have monkeys and apes?

5) The main reason that Santa is so jolly is because he knows where all the bad girls live.

6) I went to a bookstore and asked the saleswoman, "Where's the self-help section?" She said if she told me, it would defeat the purpose.

7) What if there were no hypothetical questions?

8) If a deaf child signs swear words, does his mother wash his hands with soap?

9) If someone with multiple personalities threatens to kill himself, is it considered a hostage situation?

10) Is there another word for synonym?

11) Where do forest rangers go to 'get away from it all?'

12) What do you do when you see an endangered animal eating an endangered plant?

13) If a parsley farmer is sued, can they garnish his wages?

14) Would a fly without wings be called a walk?

15) Why do they lock petrol station bathrooms? Are they afraid someone will clean them?

16) If a turtle doesn't have a shell, is he homeless or naked?

17) Can vegetarians eat animal crackers?

18) If the police arrest a mime, do they tell him he has the right to remain silent?

19) Why do they put Braille on the drive-through bank machines?

20) How do they get deer to cross the road only at those yellow road signs?

21) What was the best thing before sliced bread?

22) One nice thing about egotists, they don't talk about other people.

23) Does the Little Mermaid wear an alge bra?

24) Do infants enjoy infancy as much as adults enjoy adultery?

25) How is it possible to have a civil war?

26) If one synchronized swimmer drowns, do the rest drown too?

27) If you ate both pasta and antipasto, would you still be hungry?

28) If you try to fail, and succeed, which have you done?

29) Whose cruel idea was it for the word 'lisp' to have an 'S' in it?

30) Why is it called tourist season if we can't shoot at them?

31) Why is there an expiration date on sour cream?

32) If you spin an oriental person in a circle three times, do they become disoriented?

33) Can an atheist get insurance against acts of god?

34) If a pig loses its voice, is it disgruntled?

35) If lawyers are disbarred and clergymen defrocked, then doesn't it follow that electricians can be delighted, musicians denoted, cowboys deranged, models deposed, tree surgeons debarked, and dry cleaners depressed?

APHORISMS

An aphorism is a short, pointed sentence expressing a wise or clever observation or a general truth. Here are some gems.

1) The nicest thing about the future is that it always starts tomorrow.

2) Money will buy a fine dog, but only kindness will make him wag his tail.

3) If you don't have a sense of humor, you probably don't have any sense at all.

4) Seat belts are not as confining as wheelchairs.

5) A good time to keep your mouth shut is when you're in deep water.

6) How come it takes so little time for a child who is afraid of the dark to become a teenager who wants to stay out all night?

7) Business conventions are important because they demonstrate how many people a company can operate without.

8) Why is it that at class reunions you feel younger than everyone else looks?

9) Scratch a cat and you will have a permanent job.

10) No one has more driving ambition than the boy who wants to buy a car.

11) There are no new sins; the old ones just get more publicity.

12) There are worse things than getting a call for a wrong number at 4 A.M. It could be a right number.

13) No one ever says, "It's only a game," when their team is winning.

14) I've reached the age where the happy hour is a nap.

15) Be careful reading the fine print. There's no way you're going to like it.

16) The trouble with bucket seats is that not everybody has the same size bucket.

17) Do you realize that in about 40 years, we'll have thousands of old ladies running around with tattoos? And rap music will be the Golden Oldies!

18) Money can't buy happiness....but somehow it's more comfortable to cry in a Corvette than a Yugo.

19) After 60, if you don't wake up aching in every joint, you are probably dead!

20) Always be yourself because the people that matter don't mind, and the ones who mind, don't matter.

ANIMALS

Two chickens were too chicken to cross the road because they could see what happened to the zebra.

When the new zoo employee left the tiger cage door open and was reprimanded, he replied, "What's the big deal? Who's going to steal a tiger?"

Two sheep were standing in a field when one said, "Baaaa," and the other sheep replied, "Damn, I was going to say that."

The only member of the primate family that can fly is a hot air baboon.

Four legged animals can't dance because they have two left feet.

Why did the giraffe cross the road? It was the chicken's day off.

Why did the cow cross the road? To get to the udder side.
Why did the turtle cross the road? To get to the shell station.

Why did the sheep cross the road? To get to the baa baa shop.

Why did the dinosaur cross the road? Because chickens hadn't been invented yet.

THE BETTER HALF

What would have happened if the birth of Jesus had been attended by Three Wise Women instead of Three Wise Men? They would have asked for directions, arrived on time, helped deliver the baby, cleaned the stable, made a casserole, and brought practical gifts. But what would they have said as they left?

"Did you see the sandals Mary was wearing with that gown?"

"That baby doesn't look anything like Joseph!"

"Virgin?! Who's she kidding? I knew her in school!"

"Can you believe they allowed all those disgusting animals in there?"

"I heard that Joseph isn't even working at the moment."

"I wouldn't bet on getting your casserole dish back in a hurry!"

WOMEN WHO KNOW THEIR PLACE

Barbara Walters, of 20/20, did a story on gender roles in Kabul, Afghanistan, several years before the Afghan conflict. She noted that women customarily walked five paces behind their husbands.

She recently returned to Kabul and observed that women still walked behind their husbands. Despite the overthrow of the oppressive Taliban regime, the women are happy to maintain the old custom.

Ms. Walters approached one of the Afghani women and asked, "Why do you now seem happy with an old custom that you once tried so desperately to change?"

The woman looked Ms. Walters straight in the eyes, and without hesitation said, "Land Mines."

Moral of the story is (no matter what language you speak or where you go), behind every man, there's a smart woman!

The marriage counselor asked her client, "Did you wake up grumpy this morning?"

"No, I let him sleep in."

A man said to his wife, "Honey, let's go out and have some fun tonight."

"Okay," she replied, "Please leave the porch light on if you get home before I do."

EIGHT WORDS WITH TWO MEANINGS

1. **THINGY (thing-ee) n.**
   Female...Any part under a car's hood.
   Male...The strap fastener on a woman's bra.

2. **VULNERABLE (vul-ne-ra-bel) adj.**
   Female...Fully opening up one's self emotionally to another.
   Male...Playing football without a cup.

3. **COMMUNICATION (ko-myoo-ni-kay-shon) n.**
   Female...The open sharing of thoughts and feelings with one's partner.
   Male...Leaving a note before taking off on a fishing trip.

4. **COMMITMENT (ko-mit-ment) n.**
   Female...A desire to get married and raise a family.
   Male...Trying not to hit on other women while out with this one.

5. **ENTERTAINMENT (en-ter-tayn-ment) n.**
   Female...A good movie, concert, play or book.
   Male...Anything that can be done while drinking beer.

6. **FLATULENCE (flach-u-lens) n.**
   Female...An embarrassing by-product of indigestion.
   Male...A source of entertainment, self-expression, male bonding.

7. **MAKING LOVE (may-king luv) n.**
   Female...This greatest expression of intimacy a couple can achieve.
   Male...Call it whatever you want, just as long as we do it.

8. **REMOTE CONTROL** (ri-moht kon-trohl) n.
   Female...A device for changing from one TV channel to another.
   Male...A device for scanning through all 375 channels every five minutes.

AND

He said...I don't know why you wear a bra; you've got nothing to put in it.
She said...You wear pants don't you?

He said...What have you been doing with all the grocery money I gave you?

Quips, Quotes, Zingers & One Liners

She said...Turn sideways and look in the mirror?

He said...Why are married women heavier than single women?
She said...Single women come home, see what's in the fridge and go to bed. Married women come home, see what's in bed and go to the fridge.

BLONDES

SHE WAS SOOOOO BLONDE...

- She thought a quarterback was a refund.

- She thought General Motors was in the army.

- She thought Meow Mix was a CD for cats.

- When she went to the airport and saw a sign that said, "Airport Left," she turned around and went home.

- She thought if she spoke her mind, she'd be speechless.

- She thought that she could not use her AM radio in the evening.

- She had a shirt that said "TGIF," which she thought stood for "This Goes In Front."

- She sold the car for gas money.

- She took the ruler to bed to see how long she slept.

- She sent a fax with a stamp on it.

- She tripped over a cordless phone.

- She spent 20 minutes looking at the orange juice can because it said, "Concentrate."

~~~

How do you confuse a blonde?
Put her in a round room and tell her to sit in the corner.

~~~

Bambi, a blonde in her fourth year as a UCLA freshman, sat in her U.S. government class. The professor asked Bambi if she knew what Roe vs. Wade was about. Bambi pondered the question and then finally said, "That was the decision George Washington had to make before he crossed the Delaware."

~~~

What did the blonde ask her doctor when he told her she was pregnant?
Is it mine?

~~~

Quips, Quotes, Zingers & One Liners

She told me to meet her at the corner of "WALK" and "DON'T WALK".

~~~

Under "Education" on her job application, she put "Hooked on Phonics".

~~~

At the bottom of an application where it says "Sign here," she wrote "Sagittarius."

~~~

A young ventriloquist is touring the clubs and one night he's doing a show in a town in Essex.

With his dummy on his knee, he starts going through his usual dumb blonde jokes when a blonde woman in the fourth row stands on her chair and starts shouting, "I've heard enough of your stupid blonde jokes. What makes you think you can stereotype women that way? What does the color of a person's hair have to do with her worth as a human being? It's guys like you who keep women from reaching our full potential. Because you and your kind continue to perpetuate and discriminate against not only blondes, but women in general....and all in the name of humour."

The embarrassed ventriloquist begins to apologize and the blonde yells, "You stay out of this mister! I'm talking to that little shit sitting on your knee."

~~~

FOOTBALL AND THE BLONDE

Of all the blonde jokes, this one has to be the best...because it makes football make sense.

A guy took his blonde girlfriend to her first football game. They had great seats right behind their team's bench. After the game, he asked her how she liked it. "Oh, I really liked it," she replied, "especially the tight pants and all the big muscles, but I just couldn't understand why they were killing each other over 25 cents."

Dumbfounded, her boyfriend asked, "What do you mean?"

"Well, they flipped a coin, one team got it and then for the rest of the game all they kept screaming was 'Get the quarterback!   Get the quarterback!' I'm like, helloooo? It's only 25 cents???"

~~~

Did you hear about the blonde couple who were found frozen to death in their car at a drive-in movie theatre?
They went to see Closed For The Winter.

~~~

A married couple were asleep when the phone rang at 2 in the morning. The blonde wife picked up the phone, listened a moment and said, "How should I know that's 200 miles from here!" and hung up.

The husband said, "Who was that?"

The wife said, "I don't know, some woman wanting to know if the coast is clear."

~~~

A blonde suspects her boyfriend of cheating on her, so she goes out and buys a gun. She goes to his apartment unexpectedly and when she opens the door she finds him in the arms of a redhead.

Well, the blonde is really angry. She opens her purse to take out the gun, and as she does so, she is overcome with grief. She takes the gun and puts it to her head. The boyfriend yells, "No, honey, don't do it!!!"

The blonde replies, "Shut up, you're next!"

~~~

Two blondes met up for coffee. One said, "Wasn't yesterday's blackout terrible? I was stuck in an elevator for three hours!"

"That's nothing," said the other blonde, "I was left standing on an escalator for three hours!"

~~~

Two blondes are walking down the street. One notices a compact on the sidewalk and leans down to pick it up. She opens it, looks in the mirror and says, "Hmmm, this person looks familiar."

The second blonde says, "Here, let me see!" So the first blonde hands her the compact.

The second one looks in the mirror and says, "You dummy, it's me!"

~~~

An attractive blonde from Cork, Ireland arrived at the casino. She seemed a little intoxicated and bet twenty-thousand Euros on a single roll of the dice.

She said, "I hope you don't mind, but I feel much luckier when I'm completely nude." With that, she stripped from the neck down, rolled the dice and with an Irish brogue yelled, "Come on, baby, Mama needs new clothes!"

As the dice came to a stop, she jumped up and down and squealed, "YES! YES! I WON, I WON!"

She hugged each of the dealers and then picked up her winnings and her clothes and quickly departed.

The dealers stared at each other dumbfounded. Finally, one of them asked, "What did she roll?"

The other answered, "I don't know, I thought you were watching."

Moral of the story....not all Irish are drunks, not all blonds are dumb, but all men....are men.

~~~

She tried to put M&M's in alphabetical order.

She studied for a blood test

When she missed bus #44, she took bus #22 twice instead.

When she heard that 90% of all crimes occur around the home, she moved.

~~~

Last year, I replaced all the windows in my house with that expensive double-pane, energy-efficient kind and today I got a call from the contractor who installed them. He was complaining that the work had been completed a whole year ago and I still hadn't paid for them.

Just because I'm blonde doesn't mean that I am automatically stupid. So, I told him just what his fast talking sales guy had told me last year; that in ONE YEAR these windows would pay for themselves!

"Helloooo? It's been a year!" I told him.

There was silence at the other end of the line so I finally just hung up. He never called back. I bet he felt like a complete idiot.

~~~

A young woman in Toronto was so depressed that she decided to end her life by throwing herself into Lake Ontario. She went down to the docks and was about to leap into the frigid water when a handsome young sailor saw her teetering on the edge of the pier, crying. He took pity on her and said, "Look, you have so much to live for. I'm off to Europe in the morning and if you like, I can stow you away on my ship. I'll take good care of you and bring you food every day."

Moving closer, he slipped his arm around her shoulder and added, "I'll keep you happy and you'll keep me happy."

The girl nodded yes. After all, what did she have to lose? Perhaps a fresh start in Europe would give her life new meaning. That night, the sailor brought her aboard and hid her in a lifeboat. From then on, every night he brought her three sandwiches, some bottled water and a piece of fruit, and they had passionate sex until dawn.

Three weeks later, during a routine inspection, she was discovered by the Captain. "What are you doing here?" the Captain asked.

"I have an arrangement with one of the sailors," she explained. "I get food and a trip to Europe, and he's screwing me."

"He certainly is," the Captain said, "This is the Toronto Island Ferry."

~~~

A blonde was bragging about her knowledge of state capitals. She proudly says, "Go ahead, ask me, I know all of them."

A friend says, "Okay, what's the capital of Wisconsin?"

The blonde replies, "Oh, that's easy. W."

~~~

A woman phoned her blonde neighbor and said, "Close your curtains the next time you and your husband are having sex. The whole street was watching and laughing at you yesterday."

To which the blonde replied, "Well, the jokes on you because I wasn't even at home yesterday."

~~~

What do you call a blonde behind a steering wheel?
Airbag.

Why is it good to have a blonde passenger?
You get to park in the handicap zone.

What do you do if a blonde throws a grenade at you?
Pull the pin and throw it back.

What do you call it when a blonde dyes her hair brunette?
Artificial intelligence.

What did the blonde say when she opened the box of Cheerios?
"Honey, look at this – doughnut seeds!"

Why should blondes never be given coffee breaks?
It takes too long to retrain them.

RIVER WALK

There's this blonde out for a walk. She comes to a river and sees another blonde on the opposite bank. "Yoo-hoo!" she shouts, "How can I get to the other side?"

The second blonde looks up the river, then down the river and shouts back, "You ARE on the other side."

AT THE DOCTOR'S OFFICE

A gorgeous young redhead goes into the doctor's office and says that her body hurt wherever she touched it.

"Impossible!" says the doctor, "Show me."

The redhead took her finger, pushed on her left breast and screamed, then she pushed her elbow and screamed in even more pain. She pushed her knee and screamed, likewise she pushed her ankle and screamed. Everywhere she touched made her scream.

The doctor said, "You're not really a redhead, are you?"

"Well, no," she said, "I'm actually a blonde."

"I thought so," the doctor said, "your finger is broken."

KNITTING

A highway patrolman pulled alongside a speeding car on the freeway. Glancing at the car, he was astonished to see that the blonde behind the wheel was knitting! Realizing that she was oblivious to his flashing lights and siren, the trooper cranked down his window, turned on his bullhorn and yelled, "PULL OVER!"

"NO!" the blonde yelled back, "IT'S A SCARF!"

BLONDE ON THE SUN

A Russian, an American, and a Blonde were talking one day. The Russian said, "We were the first in space!"

The American said, "We were the first on the moon!"

The Blonde said, "So what? We're going to be the first on the sun!"

The Russian and the American looked at each other and shook their heads. "You can't land on the sun, you idiot! You'll burn up!" said the Russian.

To which the Blonde replied, "We're not stupid, you know, we're going at night!"

IN A VACUUM

A blonde was playing Trivial Pursuit one night. It was her turn. She rolled the dice and she landed on Science and Nature. Her question was, "If you are in a vacuum and someone calls your name, can you hear it?"

She thought for a time and then asked, "Is it on or off?"

FINALLY, THE BLONDE JOKE TO END ALL BLONDE JOKES

A girl was visiting her blonde friend, who had acquired two new dogs, and asked her what their names were. The blonde responded by saying that one was named Rolex and one was named Timex.

Her friend said, "Whoever heard of someone naming dogs like that?"

"HELLLOOOOO....," answered the blonde, "They're watch dogs!"

STAY!!!

I pulled into the crowded parking lot at the Super Wal-Mart Shopping Centre and rolled down the car windows to make sure my Labrador Retriever pup had fresh air.

She was stretched full-out on the back seat and I wanted to impress upon her that she must remain there! I walked to the curb backward, pointing my finger at the car and saying emphatically, "Now you stay. Do you hear me? Stay! Stay!"

The driver of a nearby car, a pretty blonde young lady, gave me a strange look and said, "Why don't you just put it in park?"

~~~

A Sheriff in a small town in Texas walks out in the street and sees a blonde haired cowboy coming toward him with nothing on him but his cowboy hat, his gun and his boots. He arrests him for indecent exposure. As he is locking him up, he asks, "Why in the world are you walking around like this?"

The cowboy says, "Well, it's like this Sheriff.....I was in this bar down the road and this pretty little redhead asks me to go out to her motor home with her. So I did.

We go inside and she pulls off her top and asks me to pull off my shirt....so I did.

Then she pulls off her skirt and asks me to pull off my pants....so I did.

Then she pulls off her panties and asks me to pull off my shorts....so I did.

Then she gets on the bed and looks at me kind of sexy and says, "Now go to town cowboy..."

"And here I am."

~~~

Returning home from work, a blonde was shocked to find her house ransacked and burglarized. She telephoned the police at once and reported the crime. The police dispatcher broadcast the call on the radio, and a K-9 unit, patrolling nearby was the first to respond. As the K-9 officer approached the house with his dog on a leash, the blonde ran out on the porch, shuddered at the sight of the cop and his dog, then sat down on the steps. Putting her face in her hands, she moaned, "I come home to find all my possessions stolen. I call the police for help, and what do they do? They send me a *blind* policeman."

~~~

A man entered the bus with both his front pockets full of golf balls and sat down next to a beautiful blonde. The puzzled blonde kept looking at him and his bulging pockets.

Finally, after many such glances from her, he said, "It's golf balls."

Nevertheless, the blonde continued to look at him for a very long time deeply thinking about what he had said.

After several minutes, not being able to contain her curiosity any longer, asked, "Does it hurt as much as tennis elbow?"

~~~

A blonde police officer stopped a blonde driver and asked for identification. The blonde driver hunted around in her purse but couldn't find her license. "Sorry officer," she said, "I must have left it at home."

"Well, do you have any form of identification on you?" asked the blonde officer.

The blonde driver took out a mirror and said, "I do have this picture of me."

The blonde officer took the mirror and looked into it. "I'm sorry," she said, "If I had known you were a police officer, I wouldn't have stopped you."

~~~

Why did the blonde put lipstick on her forehead?
Because she was trying to make up her mind.

What do you call an eternity?
Four blondes at a four-way stop.

How do you confuse a blonde?
You don't. They're born that way.

Why do blondes hate M&M's?
They're too hard to peel.

What do you call twenty blondes in a freezer?
Frosted Flakes.

Why did the blonde tiptoe past the medicine cabinet?
She didn't want to wake the sleeping pills.

How do you get a blonde to marry you?
Tell her she is pregnant.

Why did the blonde climb over the glass wall?
To see what was on the other side.

~~~

A blonde walks into a library and says, "Can I have a burger and fries?"
The librarian says, "I'm sorry, this is a library."
So the blonde whispers, "Can I have a burger and fries?"

~~~

Two blondes are headed to New York. Two hours into the flight the pilot gets on the intercom and says, "Sorry folks, we just lost an engine. Don't panic, we have three more engines, it's gonna take us an hour longer to get there."

A half hour later the pilot gets back on the intercom and says, "Sorry folks, we just lost another engine. It's okay, we have two more engines, it's just gonna take us an extra ninety minutes to get there."

One of the blondes turns to her friend and says, "Dammit! It we lose the last two engines we'll be up here all day."

THE BOSS

The man who can smile when things go wrong, has found a scapegoat.

I'm not bossy. I just know what you should be doing.

TEN BEST THINGS TO SAY IF YOU GET CAUGHT SLEEPING AT YOUR DESK

10.   "They told me at the blood bank this might happen."

9.   "This is just a 15 minute power-nap like they raved about in that time management course you sent me to."

8.   "Whew! Guess I left the top off the White-Out. You probably got here just in time!"

7.   "I wasn't sleeping. I was meditating on the mission statement and envisioning a new paradigm."

6.   "I was testing my keyboard for drool resistance."

5.   "I was doing a highly specific Yoga exercise to relieve work-related stress.   Are you discriminatory toward people who practice Yoga?"

4.   "Why did you interrupt me? I had almost figured out a solution to our biggest problem."

3.   "The coffee machine is broken."

2.   "Someone must've put decaf in the wrong pot."

And the #1 best thing to say if you get caught sleeping at your desk is...

1.   "...in Jesus' name, Amen."

"I'm very sorry," the boss told an employee, "But if I let you take a two-hour lunch today, every other worker whose wife gives birth to quadruplets will want one too."

Quips, Quotes, Zingers & One Liners
47

40 WAYS TO SAY "VERY GOOD"

1. That's the best you've ever done!
2. You're on the right track now.
3. SENSATIONAL!
4. You are very good at that.
5. I knew you could do it.
6. PERFECT!
7. Best yet.
8. I'm happy to see you working like that.
9. You're really going to town.
10. TREMENDOUS!
11. You've mastered that.
12. I sure am happy you're my student.
13. You remembered.
14. You've got that down pat!
15. SUPERB!
16. Good thinking!
17. I've never seen anyone do it better.
18. I'm very proud of you.
19. CLEVER!
20. Way to go.
21. Now you have the hang of it.
22. Congratulations, you got it right.
23. I'm proud of the way you worked today.
24. That's quite an improvement.
25. FANTASTIC!
26. You're learning fast.
27. I couldn't have done it better myself.
28. You really made being a teacher fun.
29. You haven't missed a thing.
30. WONDERFUL!
31. Nothing can stop you now.
32. Nice going.
33. Now that's what I call a fine job.
34. MARVELOUS!
35. Right on!
36. You must have been practicing.
37. Dynamite!
38. Well look at you go!
39. TERRIFIC!
40. You outdid yourself today.

Quips, Quotes, Zingers & One Liners

BUMPER STICKERS

Sometimes I pee when I laugh	One good thing about Alzheimer's, *you can hide your own Easter eggs.*
I'm so old...all my friends in heaven will think I didn't make it.	**Birthdays are good for you.** The more you have, the longer you live.
One good thing about Alzheimer's... *You get to meet new people everyday.*	**It ain't the age.** **It's the darn mileage.**
SUPPORT BINGO **Keep Grandma off the streets.**	When did my wild oats... turn to prunes and bran?

I'm not losing my hair...
I'm getting more head.

Grow your own dope. PLANT A MAN!	*Kiss Kiss Kiss* *Still no prince*	If the shoe fits, buy one in every color.
I want to be Barbie – that bitch has everything!	*A lady doesn't need a man to make her happy, but a maid is essential.*	I DON'T REPEAT GOSSIP, SO LISTEN CAREFULLY...
GOOD GIRLS GO TO HEAVEN; BAD GIRLS GO TO PARIS...ROME...	**A man's home is his castle until the queen arrives home.**	IF MAMA AIN'T HAPPY, AIN'T NOBODY HAPPY.

Inside me is a thin woman screaming to get out – I can usually keep the bitch quiet with chocolate.	I FIND IT HELPS TO ORGANIZE CHORES INTO CATEGORIES: THINGS I WON'T DO NOW THINGS I WON'T DO LATER THINGS I'LL NEVER DO...

Any woman looking for a husband, obviously has not had one.	HOUSEHOLD HINT: *Stop dusting and you can use your coffee tables as a message board.*	**I get my summer glow from a bottle. It says 'Zinfandel.'**

BUREAUCRACY

OH NOAH?

In the year 2007, the lord came unto Noah, who was now living in California, and said, "Once again, the earth has become wicked and over-populated, and I see the end of all flesh before me. Build another Ark and save 2 of every living thing along with a few good humans."

He gave Noah the blueprints, saying, "You have 6 months to build the Ark before I will start the unending raid for 40 days and 40 nights."

Six months later, the Lord looked down and saw Noah weeping in his yard, but no Ark.

"Noah!" he roared, "I'm about to start the rain! Where is the Ark?"

"Forgive me, Lord," begged Noah, "but things have changed. I needed a building permit. I've been arguing with the inspector about the need for a sprinkler system. My neighbors claim that I've violated the neighborhood zoning laws by building the Ark in my yard and exceeding the height limitations. We had to go to the Development Appeal Board for a decision.

Then the Department of Transportation demanded a bond be posted for the future costs of moving power lines and other overhead obstructions, to clear the passage for the Ark's move to the sea. I told them that the sea would be coming to us, but they would hear nothing of it.

Getting the wood was another problem. There's a ban on cutting local trees in order to save the spotted owl. I tried to convince the environmentalists that I needed the wood to save the owls – but no go!

When I started gathering the animals, an animal rights group sued me. They insisted that I was confining wild animals against their will. They argued the accommodation was too restrictive, and it was cruel and inhumane to put so many animals in a confined space.

Then the EPA ruled that I couldn't build the Ark until they'd conducted an environmental impact study on your proposed flood.

I'm still trying to resolve the complaint with the Human Rights Commission on how many minorities I'm supposed to hire for my building crew.

Immigration and Naturalization is checking the green-card status of most of the people who want to work.

The trades unions say I can't use my sons. They insist I have to hire only Union workers with Ark-building experience.

To make matters worse, the IRS seized all my assets, claiming I'm trying to leave the country illegally with endangered species. So, forgive me, Lord but it would take at least 10 years for me to finish this Ark."

Suddenly the skies cleared, the sun began to shine, and a rainbow stretched across the sky.

Noah looked up in wonder and asked, "You mean you're not going to destroy the world?"

"No," said the Lord, "the government beat me to it!"

Committee:
A group of the unwilling, picked by the unfit, to do the unnecessary.

Committee:
A body that keeps minutes and wastes hours.

Teamwork means having someone else to blame.

CHURCH

LET US HELP YOU STUDY FOR YOUR FINAL EXAMS	Adam blamed Eve Eve blamed the snake and the snake didn't have a leg to stand on
Happy Easter to our Christian Friends *Happy Passover to our Jewish Friends* *To our atheist Friends, Good Luck*	We are the **SOUL Agents** in this area!

THIS MEEK...
shall inherit the earth
If it's all right with you!

An isolated monastery was inhabited by an order of monks who communicated with each other solely by chanting. Every morning, they would gather in the chapel and the Abbot would chant, "Good morning, assembled brethren." And the monks would change back, "Good morning, Father Abbot."

But one morning, a maverick monk instead chanted, "Good evening, Father Abbot."

The abbot was not amused. Glaring at the monks, he declared, "Someone chanted evening."

~~~

The Mother Superior called all the nuns together and announced, "I must tell you all something. We have a case of gonorrhoea in the convent."

"Thank heavens!" said an elderly nun at the back of the room, "I'm so tired of Chardonnay."

~~~

A young man asked his father, a church minister, if he could borrow the family car.

"Not until you get your hair cut," said the father.

"What's your problem?" asked the son. "Moses had long hair, so did Samson and even Jesus."

"That's true," said the father, "And they also walked everywhere."

~~~

One day, the Devil challenged God to a baseball game between Hell and Heaven.

"You don't have a chance," said God, "I have Babe Ruth, Mickey Mantle and all the greatest players up here."

"Yes," grinned the Devil, "but I have all the umpires."

~~~

What do you get when you cross an atheist with a Jehovah's *Witness?*
Somebody knocking on your door for no apparent reason.

You say you don't know where Jesus is.

God's last name is not 'Dammit'

ECONOMICS

NEW STOCK MARKET TERMS

CEO: Chief Embezzlement Officer

CFO: Corporate Fraud Officer

Bull Market: A random market movement causing an investor to mistake himself for a financial genius.

Bear Market: A six to 18 month period when the kids get no allowance, the wife gets no jewellery and the husband gets no sex.

Value Investing: The art of buying low and selling lower.

P/E Ratio: The percentage of investors wetting their pants as the market keeps crashing.

Broker: What my broker has made me.

Standard & Poor: Your life in a nutshell.

Stock Analyst: Idiot who just downgraded your stock.

Stock Split: When your ex-wife and her lawyer split your assets equally between themselves.

Financial Planner: A guy whose phone has been disconnected.

Market Correction: The day after you buy stocks.

Cash Flow: The movement your money makes as it disappears down the toilet.

Yahoo: What you yell after selling it to some poor sucker for $240 per share.

Windows: What you jump out of when you're the sucker who bought Yahoo at $240 per share.

Institutional Investor: Past year investor who is now locked up in a nuthouse.

Profit: An archaic word no longer in use.

After filing their personal tax returns by April 30th, many Canadians will again receive a tax refund. This is indeed a very exciting program, and I'll explain it in a Q&A format.

Q: What is a tax refund payment?
A: It's money that the federal government will send to taxpayers.

Q: Where will the government get the money?
A: From taxpayers.

Q: So the government is giving me back my own money?
A: Only a smidgen of it.

Q: What is the purpose of this payment?
A: The plan is for you to use the money to purchase a high-definition TV set, thus stimulating the economy.

Q: But isn't that stimulating the economy of China?
A: Shut up.

Conclusion:

If you spend the stimulus money at Wal-Mart, the money will go to China or Sri Lanka.

If you spend it on gasoline, your money will go to the Arabs.

If you purchase a computer, it will go to India, Taiwan or China.

If you purchase fruit and vegetables, it will go to Mexico, Honduras and Guatemala.

If you buy an efficient car, it will go to Japan or Korea.

If you purchase useless stuff, it will go to Taiwan.

If you pay your credit cards off, or buy stock, it will go to management bonuses and they will hide it offshore.

~~~

Economy: Denying ourselves a necessity today in order to buy a luxury tomorrow.

ETHNIC HUMOUR

Quips, Quotes, Zingers & One Liners

No! We don't sell love making aids.

~~~

A Frenchman staying at a hotel in New York rang room service for some pepper.

"Black pepper or white pepper?" asked the voice on the other end.

"No," said the Frenchman. "Toilet pepper!"

~~~

I saw Abdul shaking out a rug and asked, "Won't it start?"

~~~

Two Mexican detectives were investigating the murder of Juan Gonzalez.

"How was he killed?" asked one detective.

"With a golf gun," the other detective replied.

"A golf gun?! What is a golf gun?"

"I don't know, but it sure made a hole in Juan."

~~~

JEWISH HUMOR

You may remember the old Jewish Catskill comics of Vaudeville days, Shecky Green, Milton Berle, Henny Youngman, and others? You've probably heard of them before, but don't you miss their humor if you are old enough. Not one single swear word in their comedy.

A car hit an elderly Jewish man. The paramedic says, "Are you comfortable?"
The man says, "I make a good living."

I just got back from a pleasure trip.
I took my mother-in-law to the airport.

I've been in love with the same woman for 49 years!
It my wife ever finds out, she'll kill me.

What are three words a woman never wants to hear when she's making love?
"Honey, I'm home!"

Someone stole all my credit cards, but I won't be reporting it. The thief spends less than my wife did.

My wife and I went back to the hotel where we spent our wedding night, only this time I stayed in the bathroom and cried.

My wife and I went to a hotel where we got a waterbed.
My wife called it the Dead Sea.

I was just in London; there is a six-hour time difference.
I'm still confused. When I go to dinner, I feel sexy.
When I go to bed, I feel hungry.

The doctor gave a man six months to live. The man couldn't pay his bill, so the doctor gave him another six months.

The doctor called Mrs. Cohen saying, "Mrs. Cohen, your check came back."
Mrs. Cohen answered, "So did my arthritis!"

Doctor: "You'll live to be 60!"
Patient: "I AM 60!"
Doctor: "See! What did I tell you?"

A doctor held a stethoscope up to a man's chest. The man asks, "Doc, how do I stand?"
The doctor says, "That's what puzzles me!"

Patient: "I have a ringing in my ears."
Doctor: "Don't answer!"

A drunk was in front of a judge. The judge says, "You've been brought here for drinking."
The drunk says, "Okay, let's get started."

Why do Jewish divorces cost so much?
They're worth it.

Why do Jewish men die before their wives?
They want to.

My parents didn't want to move to Florida, but they turned sixty and that's the law.

Chutzpah is a Yiddish word meaning gall, brazen, nerve, effrontery, sheer guts plus arrogance. Leo Rosten writes, "No other word, and no other language can do it justice."

~~~

A little old lady sold pretzels on a street corner for 25 cents each. Every day a young man would leave his office building at lunch time, and as he passed the pretzel stand, he would leave her a quarter, but never take a pretzel.

This went on for more than three years. The two of them never spoke. One day, as the young man passed the old lady's stand and left his quarter as usual, the pretzel lady spoke to him, without blinking an eye, she said, "They're 35 cents now."

~~~

A young boy approached his father at the end of his first day of Hebrew school, "Father, I need five dollars to buy a used textbook for school."

"Four dollars?" the father replied. "What do you need three dollars for?"

~~~

The teacher addressed his class, 'I'll give five dollars to anybody who can name the most famous person in the history of the world."

An Irish boy raised his hand and said, "St. Patrick."

"Sorry Seamus, that's not correct."

Then a French boy raised his hand and said, "Napoleon."

The teacher replied, "I'm sorry, Jean, that's not right either."

Finally, a Jewish boy raised his hand and answered, "It was Jesus Christ."

"That's right, David! You win the five dollars. Congratulations!" As the teacher was handing over the cash he said, "You know David, you being Jewish, I'm surprised you said Jesus Christ."

"Yeah, in my heart I knew it was Moses. But business is business."

~~~

The Harvard School of Medicine did a study of why Jewish women like Chinese food so much. The study revealed that this is due to the fact that Won Ton spelled backward is Not Now.

There is a big controversy on the Jewish view of when life begins. In Jewish tradition, the fetus is not considered viable until it graduates from medical school.

Q: Why don't Jewish mothers drink?
A: Alcohol interferes with their suffering.

Q: Have you seen the newest Jewish-American-Princess horror movie?
A: It's called, "Debbie Does Dishes."

Q: Why do Jewish mothers make great parole officers?
A: They never let anyone finish a sentence.

Q: What's a Jewish American Princess's favorite position?
A: Facing Bloomingdales.

~~~

A man called his mother in Florida, "Mom, how are you?"

"Not too good," said the mother. "I've been very weak."

The son said, "Why are you so weak?"

She said, "Because I haven't eaten in 38 days."

The son said, "That's terrible. Why haven't you eaten in 38 days?"

The mother answered, "Because I didn't want my mouth to be filled with food if you should call."

~~~

A Jewish boy comes home from school and tells his mother he has a part in the play. She asks, "What part is it?"

The boy says, "I play the part of a Jewish husband."

The mother scowls and says, "Go back and tell the teacher you want a speaking part."

~~~

Q: Where does a Jewish husband hide money from his wife?
A: Under the vacuum cleaner.

Q: How many Jewish mothers does it take to change a light bulb?
A: (sigh) Don't bother. I'll sit in the dark. I don't want to be a nuisance to anybody.

Short summary of every Jewish holiday:
They tried to kill us, we won, let's eat.

Did you hear about the bum who walked up to the Jewish mother on the street and said, "Lady, I haven't eaten in three days."
"Force yourself," she replied.

Q: What's the difference between a Rottweiler and a Jewish mother?
A: Eventually, the Rottweiler lets go.

Q: Why are Jewish men circumcised?
A: Because Jewish women don't like anything that isn't 20% off.

~~~

An Arab, fleeing the Taliban, desperate for water, was plodding through the Afghanistan desert when he saw something far off in the distance. Hoping to find water, he walked towards the image, only to find a little old Jewish man sitting at a card table with a bunch of neckties laid out on it. The Arab asked, "I'm dying of thirst, can I have some water?"

The Jew replied, "I don't have any water, but why don't you buy a tie? They are only $15.00. Here's one that goes very nicely with your robes."

The Arab shouted, "I don't want an overpriced tie, you idiot, I need water!"

The Jew replied, "Okay then, don't buy a tie. But to show you what a nice guy I am, I'll tell you that over that hill there, about four miles, is a nice restaurant. Walk that way, they have all the water you need."

The Arab begrudgingly thanked him, then staggered away towards the hill and eventually disappeared. Four hours later the Arab came crawling back to where the Jewish man was sitting behind his card table.

The Jew said, "I told you, about four miles over that hill. Couldn't you find it?"

The Arab rasped, "I found it all right. Your brother wouldn't let me in without a tie!"

~~~

Mona Lisa's Jewish Mother:
"After all that money your father and I spent on braces, this you call a smile?"

Christopher Columbus' Jewish Mother:
"I don't care what you've discovered, you didn't call, you didn't write."

Michelangelo's Jewish Mother:
"A ceiling you paint? Not good enough for the walls, like the other children? Do you know how hard it is to get that schmutz off the ceiling?"

Napoleon's Jewish Mother:
"You're not hiding your report card? Show me! Take your hand out of your jacket and show me!"

Abraham Lincoln's Jewish Mother:
"Again with the hat! Why can't you wear a baseball cap like the other kids?"

George Washington's Jewish Mother:
"Next time I catch you throwing money across the Potomac, you can kiss your allowance goodbye!"

Albert Einstein's Jewish Mother:
"Your senior photograph and you couldn't have done something with your hair?"

Moses' Jewish Mother:
"Desert, schmesert! Where have you really been for the last forty years?"

Bill Gates' Jewish Mother:
"It would have killed you to become a doctor?"

Bill Clinton's Jewish Mother:
"Well, at least she was a nice Jewish girl, that Monica."

~~~

A Jewish man was talking to his psychiatrist, "I had a weird dream recently. I saw my mother but then I noticed she had your face. It was so disturbing I couldn't fall back to sleep. I just lay there staring at the ceiling, thinking about it until 7 AM. I finally got up, made myself a slice of toast and some coffee, and came straight here. Can you please help me explain the meaning of my dream?"

The psychiatrist kept silent for some time and then said, "One slice of toast and coffee? Do you call that a breakfast?"

~~~

A Jewish grandmother walks into a post office to send a package to her son. The postal worker says, "This package is too heavy, you'll need another stamp."

"And that should make it lighter?" the Jewish grandmother asks.

~~~

Q: How does a Jewish kid verbally abuse his playmates?
A: "Your mama pays retail."

Q: What's the difference between a Jewish grandmother and an Italian grandmother?
A: About twenty-five pounds.

Q: What did the Jewish grandmother bank teller say to her customer?
A: You never write, you never call. You only come to see me when you need money.

Q: What is the most common disease transmitted by Jewish grandmothers?
A: Guilt.

Q: What kind of cigarettes do Jewish grandmothers smoke?
A: Gefiltered.

~~~

"Oy! I got good news and bad news about our son," Mrs. Shapiro said to her husband.

"Give me the bad news first!" Mr. Shapiro replied.

"Okay, I just found out our son is a homosexual."

"A homosexual?? What could possibly be the good news?"

"He's going with a rich doctor!"

~~~

A Jewish grandmother is at the beach with her grandson, when a tidal wave sweeps the young boy into the sea. The grandmother immediately falls to her knees and prays to God for the return of her grandson.

"Please God, I have always been a good Jew and a loving bubby. Please, please return my grandson to me."

Just as she finishes her prayer, a big wave comes and washes the boy back onto the beach, good as new. She looks up to heaven and cries, "He had a hat, too!"

~~~

A Jewish grandmother is giving directions to her grandson who is coming to visit. "Come to the front door of the building. I am in apartment 7G. With your elbow push the button next to 7G and I will buzz you in. Come inside, the elevator is on the left. With your elbow, open the elevator and get in, and with your elbow, hit seven. When you get out I am on the left. With your elbow, hit my doorbell."

"Bubby, that sounds easy. But why am I hitting all these buttons with my elbow?"

"What, you're coming empty handed?"

Q: What did the waiter ask the group of Jewish mothers?
A: Is anything okay?

Son: "Hello Mom, how are you?"
Mom: "Very well, thanks!"
Son: "Oh, sorry, I must have dialed the wrong number."

THE FAIRER SEX

New Drugs For Women

Damnitol:
Take two and the rest of the world can go to hell for up to eight full hours.

Emptynestrogen:
Suppository that eliminates melancholy and loneliness by reminding you of how awful they were as teenagers and how you couldn't wait till they moved out.

St. Momma's Wort:
Plant extract that treats mom's depression by rendering preschoolers unconscious for up to two days.

Peptobimbo:
Liquid silicone drink for single women. Two full cups swallowed before an evening out increases breast size, decreases intelligence, and prevents constipation.

Dumberol:
When taken with Peptobimbo, can cause dangerously low IQ, resulting in enjoyment of country music and pickup trucks.

Flipitor:
Increases life expectancy of commuters by controlling road rage and the urge to flip off other drivers.

Menicillin:
Potent anti-boy-otic for older women. Increases resistance to such lethal lines as, "You make me want to be a better person."

Buyagra:
Injectable stimulant taken prior to shoppin increases potency, duration and credit limit of spending spree.

Jackasspirin:
Relieves headache caused by a man who can't remember your birthday, anniversary, phone number, or to lift the toilet seat.

Anti-talksident:
A spray carried in a purse to be used on anyone too eager to share their life stories with total strangers in elevators.

Nagament:
When administered to a boyfriend or husband, provides the same irritation level as nagging him.

IF WOMEN RULED THE WORLD...

...men who design women's shoes would be forced to wear them.

...shopping would be considered an aerobic activity.

...men would HAVE to get *Playboy* for the articles because there'd be no pictures.

SHE WAS ONLY...

...a photographer's daughter, but she was really well developed.

...a road worker's daughter, but she knew how to get her asphalt.

...a barrister's daughter, but she kept a tight hold on her briefs.

...a draughtsman's daughter, but she knew where to draw the line.

...a constable's daughter, but she wouldn't let the Chief Inspector.

...a weatherman's daughter, but she had a warm front.

...a doctor's daughter, but she really knew how to operate.

...a jockey's daughter, but all the horse manure.

...an optician's daughter, but she was always making a spectacle of herself.

...a fisherman's daughter, but all the guys swallowed her lines.

...an electrician's daughter, but she was well connected.

...a bookbinder's daughter, but she knew her way between the sheets.

...a violinist's daughter, but when she took off her G-string all the boys fiddled.

...a minister's daughter, but I wouldn't put anything pastor.

...a whisky maker's daughter, but he loved her still.

FAMILY PETS

He's not mine.

Perhaps he'll move if I use my spurs.

"I TOLD YOU
NO BLEACH"

"DROP DEAD"

I'm not saying that
you're lacking in
intelligence.

It just seems as though
you are intelligence
challenged.

REMEMBER THAT
CANARY

You're not fat.
You're just undertall.

He's not heavy.
He's my brother.

He started it!

The police came to my house earlier and said my dog had chased someone on a bike. I said, "You must be joking officer, my dog hasn't got a bike."

FOR MEN ONLY

FALL CLASSES FOR MEN

Registration must be completed by – Monday, October 23rd

NOTE: Due to the complexity and difficulty level of their contents, class sizes will be limited to eight participants maximum.

Classes begin – Monday, October 30th

Class 1
How to Fill Up Ice Cube Trays – Step by Step – With Slide Presentation
Meets 4 weeks, Monday and Wednesday for 2 hours, beginning at 7:00 PM

Class 2
The Toilet Paper Roll – Does It Change Itself? Round Table Discussion
Meets 2 weeks, Saturday 12:00 for 2 hours

Class 3
Is It Possible To Urinate Using The Technique of Lifting The Seat and Avoiding the Floors, Walls and Nearby Bathtub? – Group Practice
Meets 4 weeks, Saturday 10:00 PM for 2 hours

Class 4
Fundamental Differences between The Laundry Hamper and the Floor – Pictures and Explanatory Graphics
Meets Saturday at 2:00 PM for 3 weeks

Class 5
After Dinner Dishes – Can They Levitate and Fly into the Kitchen Sink? Examples on Video
Meets 4 weeks, Tuesday and Thursday for 2 hours beginning at 7:00 PM

Class 6
Loss of Identity – Losing the Remote to Your Significant Other Help Line Support and Support Groups
Meets 4 weeks, Friday and Sunday 7:00 PM

Class 7
Learning How to Find Things – Starting with Looking in the Right Places and Not Turning the House Upside Down While Screaming Open Forum
Monday at 8:00 PM, 2 hours

Class 8
Health Watch – Bringing Her Flowers is Not Harmful to Your Health Graphics and Audio Tapes
Three nights, Monday, Wednesday, Friday at 7:00 PM for 2 hours

Class 9
Real Men Ask for Directions When Lost – Real Life Testimonials
Tuesday at 6:00 PM, location to be determined

Class 10
Is it Genetically Impossible to Sit Quietly While She Parallel Parks? Driving Simulations
4 weeks, Saturday noon, 2 hours

Class 11
Learning to Live – Basic Differences Between Mother and Wife Online Classes and Role-playing
Tuesday 7:00 PM, location to be determined

Class 12
How to be the Ideal Shopping Companion Relaxation Exercises, Meditation and Breathing Techniques
Meets 4 weeks, Tuesday and Thursday for 2 hours, beginning at 7:00 PM

Class 13
How to Fight Cerebral Atrophy – Remembering Birthdays, Anniversaries and other Important Dates, and Calling When You're Going to be Late
Cerebral Shock Therapy Sessions and Full Lobotomies Offered
Three nights, Monday, Wednesday, Friday at 7:00 PM for 2 hours

Class 14
The Stove/Oven – What It Is and How It Is Used Live Demonstration
Tuesday at 6:00 PM, location to be determined

Upon completion of any of the above courses, diplomas will be issued to the survivors.

Quips, Quotes, Zingers & One Liners
91

A man sticks his head into a barbershop and asks, "How long before I can get a haircut?"

The barber looks around the busy shop and says, "About an hour." The man leaves.

A few days later, the same man sticks his head in the door and asks, "How long before I can get a haircut?"

The barber looks around at the busy shop and says, "Same as the other day, about an hour." The man leaves.

A week later the same man sticks his head in the shop and asks, "How long before I can get a haircut?"

The barber looks around the shop, which isn't very busy and, and says, "About ten minutes." The man leaves.

The barber looks over at a friend and says, "Hey, follow that guy and see where he goes. He keeps asking how long he has to wait for a haircut, but never comes back."

A little while later the friend comes back into the barbershop chuckling. The barber asks, "So where did he go when he left here?"

"Your house!" the friend answers.

~~~

After a few too many visits to the 'Pleasure Parlour', a chap called Mike notices green lumps on his willy. So off he goes to the doctor.

The doctor explains, "You know how wrestlers and rugby players get cauliflower ears?"

"Yes," says Bill, nodding seriously.

"Well," says the doctor, "You've got Brothel sprouts."

FRIENDS

If friends were flowers, I'd pick you.

Friendship is the wine of life

It takes a long time to grow an old friend.

You'll always be my best friend, you know too much.

Friends are the family you choose for yourself.

And remember, good friends are like stars,
You don't always see them
But you always know they are there!!!

Me and you is friends.
You smile, I smile...
You hurt, I hurt...
You cry, I cry...
You jump off a bridge, I gonna miss your emails.

We'll be friends until we are old and senile.
Then we'll be NEW friends.

A friend will stop you from overreacting.
A best friend will walk beside you giggling, "Someone is gonna get it!"

GOVERNMENT

Below is some helpful advice on how to best help the Canadian economy by spending your tax funding wisely:

Instead, keep the money in Canada by:

1) Spending it at yard sales, or
2) Going to hockey games, or
3) Spending it on prostitutes, or
4) Beer or
5) Tattoos

These are the only 'truly' Canadian businesses still operating.

Conclusion:

Go to a hockey game with a tattooed prostitute that you met at a yard sale and drink beer all day!

THE BAILOUT MASCOT

The government today announced that it is changing its national symbol to a CONDOM because it more accurately reflects the government's political stance. A condom allows for inflation, halts production, destroys the next generation, and protects a bunch of pricks, gives you a sense of security while you're actually being screwed. It just doesn't get more accurate than that!

~~~

A penny saved is obviously the result of a government oversight.

Be thankful we're not getting all the government we're paying for.

~~~

I just received my tax return for 2011 from Revenue Canada. It puzzles me! They are questioning how many dependents I claimed. I guess it was because of my response to the line 'List All Dependents'. I replied:

2 million Native Indians, 1 million crack heads, 7.3 million unemployed people, 100,000 people in prisons, half of Haiti, 105 persons in the Federal Senate, 308 Members of Parliament.

Evidently, this is NOT an acceptable answer. I keep asking myself, who did I miss?

~~~

So you're a senior citizen and the government says no healthcare for you. What do you do? Our plan gives anyone 65 years or older a gun and four bullets. You are allowed to shoot two politicians and two bureaucrats. Of course, this means you will be sent to prison where you will get three meals per day, a roof over your head, and all the healthcare you need! New teeth, no problem. Need glasses, great. New hip, knees, lungs, heart? All covered. And who will be paying for all of this? The same government that just told you that you are too old for healthcare. Plus, because you are a prisoner, you don't have to pay any income taxes anymore. Is this a great country, or what?!

~~~

Due to the current financial restraints, the light at the end of the tunnel will be turned off until further notice.

~~~

The Medical Profession speaks out on the Financial Bail Out Package.

The Allergists voted to scratch it, and the Dermatologists advised not to make any rash moves.

The Gastroenterologists had sort of a gut feeling about it, but the Neurologists thought the Administration had a lot of nerve, and the Obstetricians felt they were all laboring under a misconception.

The Ophthalmologists considered the idea short-sighted, the Pathologists yelled, 'Over my dead body!' while the Pediatricians said, 'Oh, grow up!'

The Psychiatrists thought the whole idea was madness, the Radiologists could see right through it, and the Surgeons decided to wash their hands of the whole thing.

The Internists thought it was a bitter pill to swallow, and the Plastic Surgeons said, 'This puts a whole new face on the matter.'

The Podiatrists thought it was a step forward, but the Urologists felt the scheme wouldn't hold water.

The Anesthesiologists thought the whole idea was a gas; and the Cardiologists didn't have the heart to say no.

In the end, the Proctologists left the decision up to some a**holes in Washington.

~~~

THE SCIENCE OF GOVERNANCE

A major research institution has announced the discovery of the heaviest element yet known to science – "governmentium."

It has one neutron, 12 assistant neutrons, 75 deputy neutrons and 111 assistant deputy neutrons for an atomic mass of 312. These 312 particles are held together by forces called "morons" that are further surrounded by vast quantities of lepton-like subparticles called "peons."

Governmentium has no electrons and is therefore inert. It can be detected, however, since it impedes every reaction it comes into contact with.

A tiny amount of governmentium can take a reaction that normally occurs in seconds and slow it to the point where it takes days.

Governmentium has a normal shelf life of three years. It doesn't decay but "reorganizes," a process where assistant deputy neutrons and deputy neutrons change places. This process actually causes it to grow as, in the confusion, some morons become neutrons, thereby forming isodopes.

This phenomenon of "moron promotion" has led to some speculation that governmentium forms whenever sufficient morons meet in concentration, forming "cricital morass." Researchers believe that with governmentium, the more you reorganize, the morass you cover.

~~~

A FINE IS A TAX FOR DOING WRONG. A TAX IS A FINE FOR DOING WELL.

HELPFUL

AMAZINGLY SIMPLE HOME REMEDIES

1) A mouse trap placed on top of your alarm clock, will prevent you from rolling over and going back to sleep after you hit the snooze button.
2) If you have a bad cough, take a large dose of laxatives, then you will be afraid to cough.
3) Clumsy? Avoid cutting yourself while slicing vegetables by getting someone else to hold them while you chop away.
4) Avoid arguments with the Mrs. about lifting the toilet seat by simply using the sink.
5) For high blood pressure sufferers, simply cut yourself and bleed for a few minutes, thus reducing the pressure in your veins. Remember to use a timer.
6) Have a bad toothache? Smash your thumb with a hammer and you will forget about the toothache.

~~~

Sometimes, we just need to remember what the rules of life really are. You only need two tools – WD-40 and Duct Tape. If it doesn't move and should, use the WD-40. If it shouldn't move but does, use the Duct Tape.

~~~

Remember:
Everyone seems normal until you get to know them.
Never pass up an opportunity to go to the bathroom.
If you woke up breathing, congratulations! You get another chance.

And finally, be really nice to your family and friends, you never know when you might need them to empty your bedpan.

~~~

Dear Abby,

My husband is a liar and a cheat. He has cheated on me from the beginning, and, when I confront him, he denies everything. What's worse, everyone knows that he cheats on me. It is so humiliating. Also, since he lost his job five years ago, he hasn't even looked for a new one.

All he does all day is smoke cigars, cruise around and chew the fat with his buddies while I have to pay the bills. Since our daughter went away to college he doesn't even pretend to like me and hints that I may be a lesbian. What should I do?

Signed,
Clueless

Dear Clueless,

Grow up and dump him. Good grief, woman. You don't need him anymore. You're a United States Senator from New York. Act like one.

~~~

By following the simple advice I heard on a medical TV show, I have finally found deep inner peace. A doctor proclaimed the way to achieve inner peace is to finish all the things you have started.

So, I looked around my house to see things I started and hadn't finished and, before leaving the house this morning I finished off:

- A bottle of Merlot
- A bottle of Shhhardonay
- A bodle of Baileys
- A butle of vocka
- A pockage of Prunflies
- The mainder of bot Prozic and Valum scriptins
- The res of the tchesescke an a box a choqolettss.

Yu haf no idr who bloudee gud I fel. Peas send is orn to ennun yu fee ar in ned of inr pece.

~~~

There should be support groups for women who can't put their dishes in the dishwasher dirty.

~~~

Colonoscopies are no joke, but these comments during the exam were quite humorous...A physician claimed that the following are actual comments made by his patients (predominately male) while he was performing their colonoscopies:

1) Take it easy, Doc. You're boldly going where no man has gone before!
2) Find Amelia Earhart yet?
3) Can you hear me NOW?
4) Are we there yet? Are we there yet? Are we there yet?
5) You know, in Arkansas, we're now legally married.
6) Any sign of the trapped miners, Chief?
7) You put your left hand in, you take your left hand out...
8) Hey! Now I know how a Muppet feels!
9) If your hand doesn't fit, you must quit!
10) Hey, Doc, let me know if you find my dignity.
11) You used to be an executive at Enron, didn't you?
And the best one of all...
12) Could you write a note for my wife saying that my head is not up there?

~~~

IF YOU NEED A SHOULDER TO CRY ON, PULL OFF TO THE SIDE OF THE ROAD.

~~~

YOU'VE SENT IN YOUR CHEQUE? OOPS!

Quips, Quotes, Zingers & One Liners

MIR	FRI	FRI	FRI	THU	WED	TUE
8	7	6	5	4	3	2
16	14	13	12	11	10	9
23	22	21	20	19	18	17
32	29	28	27	26	25	24
39	38	37	36	35	34	33

1) This is a special calendar which has been developed for handling rush jobs. All rush jobs are wanted yesterday. With this calendar, a client can order his work on the 7th and have it delivered on the 3rd.

2) Everyone wants his job by Friday, so there are three Fridays in every week.

3) There are eight new days at the end of the month for those end-of-the-month jobs.

4) There is no first of the month so there can't be late delivery of end-of-month jobs.

5) A 'Blue Monday' or 'Monday morning hangover' can't happen as all Mondays have been eliminated.

6) There are no bothersome non-productive Saturdays and Sundays – no compensatory leave or overtime to worry about.

7) 'Mirday' – A special day each week for performing miracles.

~~~

DIRECTORY ENQUIRIES

Caller: I'd like the number of the Argo fish Bar, please.
Operator: I'm sorry, there's no listing. Are you sure that the spelling is correct?
Caller: Well, it used to be called the Cargo Fish Bar, but the 'C' fell off.

Caller: Can you give me the telephone number for Jack?
Operator: I'm sorry, sir, I don't understand who you are talking about.
Caller: On page 1, section 5 of the user guide it clearly states that I need to unplug the machine from the AC wall socket and telephone Jack before cleaning. Now, can you give me the telephone number for Jack?
Operator: I think it means the telephone plug on the wall.

Quips, Quotes, Zingers & One Liners

Customer: I've been calling 700 – 1000 for two days and can't get through, can you help me?
Operator: Where did you get that number, sir?
Customer: It's on the door of your business
Operator: Sir, those are the hours that we are open.

On another occasion, a man making heavy breathing sounds from a phone box told a worried operator, "I haven't got a pen, so I'm steaming up the window to write the number on."

There was the caller who asked for a knitwear company in Woven.
Operator: Woven? Are you sure?
Caller: Yes, that's what it says on the label, Woven in Scotland

Caller: Does your European Breakdown Policy cover me when I am travelling in Australia?
Operator: Does the policy name give you a clue?

Caller: (enquiring about legal requirements while traveling in Europe) If I register my car in France, and then take it to England, do I have to change the steering wheel to the other side of the car?

I'D BE UNSTOPPABLE IF NOT FOR LAW ENFORCEMENT & PHYSICS

BEING MALE IS A MATTER OF BIRTH, BEING A MAN IS A MATTER OF AGE, BEING A GENTLEMAN IS A MATTER OF CHOICE

HUSBAND & WIFE

You have two choices in life. You can stay single and be miserable, or get married and wish you were dead.

At a cocktail party, one woman said to another, "Aren't you wearing your wedding ring on the wrong finger?"
"Yes, I am. I married the wrong man."

When a woman steals your husband, there is no better revenge than to let her keep him.

A little boy asked his father, "Daddy, how much does it cost to get married?"
The father replied, "I don't know, I'm still paying."

A young son asked, "Is it true Dad, that in some parts of Africa a man doesn't know his wife until he marries her?"
The dad replied, "That happens in every country, son."

Then there was a woman who said, "I never knew what real happiness was until I got married, and by then, it was too late."

Marriage is the triumph of imagination over intelligence.

Just think, if it weren't for marriage, men would go through life thinking they had no faults at all.

First guy says, "My wife's an angel!"
The second guy remarks, "You're lucky, mine's still alive."

A WOMAN'S PRAYER:

Dear Lord, I pray for Wisdom to understand a man, to Love and to forgive him, and for Patience for his moods. Because Lord, if I pray for Strength I'll just beat him to death.

~~~

A husband and wife are waiting at the bus stop with their nine children. A blind man joins them after a few minutes. When the bus arrives, they find it overloaded and only the wife and the nine kids are able to fit onto the bus. The husband and the blind man decide to walk.

After a while, the husband gets irritated by the ticking of the stick of the blind man as he taps it on the sidewalk, and says to him, "Why don't you put a piece of rubber at the end of your stick? That ticking sound is driving me crazy."

The blind man replies, "If you had put a rubber at the end of YOUR stick, we'd be riding the bus, so shut the hell up."

~~~

A couple had been married for 50 years. They were sitting at the breakfast table one morning when the wife says, "Just think, fifty years ago we were sitting here at this breakfast table together."

"I know," the old man said. "We were probably sitting here naked as a jaybird fifty years ago."

"Well," Granny snickered,"Let's relive some old times." Where upon the two stripped to the buff and sat down at the table.

"You know honey," the little old lady breathlessly replied, "My nipples are as hot for you today as they were fifty years ago."

"I wouldn't be surprised," replied Gramps. "One's in your coffee and the other is in your oatmeal."

~~~

Bigamy is having one wife or husband too many.
Manogamy is the same.

Quips, Quotes, Zingers & One Liners

MAD WIFE DISEASE

A guy was sitting quietly reading his paper when his wife walked up behind him and whacked him on the head with a magazine.

"What was that for?" he asked.

"That was for the piece of paper in your pants pocket with the name Laura Lou written on it," she replied.

"Two weeks ago when I went to the races, Laura Lou was the name of one of the horses I bet on," he explained.

"Oh honey, I'm sorry," she said, "I should have known there was a good explanation."

Three days later he was watching a ball game on TV when she walked up and hit him in the head again, this time with an iron skillet, which knocked him out cold. When he came to, he asked, "What the heck was that for?"

She replied…."Your horse called."

Everyday I live with fear but occasionally I leave her and go drag racing.

The smartest thing a man ever said was, "Yes, Dear"

BONUS COMMANDMENT STORY

A long married couple came upon a wishing well. The wife leaned over, made a wish and threw in a penny. The husband decided to make a wish too. But he leaned over too much, fell into the well, and drowned. The wife was stunned for a moment but then smiled, "It really works!"

15 THINGS TO DO AT WALMART WHILE YOUR SPOUSE IS TAKING HER SWEET TIME

1. Get 24 boxes of condoms and randomly put them in people's carts when they aren't looking.

2. Set all the alarm clocks in housewares to go off at five minute intervals.

3. Walk up to an employee and tell him/her in an official tone, "Code 3 in housewares," and see what happens.

4. Go to the Service Desk and ask to put a bag of M&M's on lay away.

5. Move a 'CAUTION – WET FLOOR' sign to a carpeted area.

6. Set up a tent in the camping department and tell other shoppers you'll invite them in only if they bring pillows from the bedding department.

7. When a clerk asks if they can help you, begin to cry and ask, "Why can't people just leave me alone?"

8. While handling guns in the hunting department ask the clerk if he knows where the antidepressants are.

9. Dart around the store suspiciously while loudly humming the theme from 'Mission Impossible.'

10. In the auto department, practice your Madonna look using different size funnels.

11. Hide in the clothing rack and when people browse through say, "PICK ME! PICK ME!"

12. When an announcement comes over the loud speaker, assume the fetal position and scream, "NO! NO! It's those voices again."

And last, but not least...

13. Go into a fitting room and yell loudly, "Hey! We're out of toilet paper in here!"

~~~

A doctor examined a woman, took the husband aside and said, "I don't like the looks of your wife at all."
"Me neither doc," said the husband, "But she's a great cook and really good with the kids."

Quips, Quotes, Zingers & One Liners
116

~~~

"Mr. Clark, I have reviewed this case very carefully," the divorce court Judge said, "And I've decided to give your wife $775 a week."
"That's very fair, your Honor," the husband said, "And every now and then, I'll try to send her a few bucks myself."

Does marriage pay for sex or is sex the cost of marriage?

After you get used to it, marriage isn't so hot – something like a hot bath.

I came home and found my wife with three nude men and said, "Well, hello, hello, hello!"
And my wife responded, "What's wrong, aren't you speaking to me?"

A tight dress and a chain-link fence have one thing in common. They protect what's inside while allowing a good view.

Definition of marriage – sleeping with the enemy.

My wife and I go together like a horse and carriage – she's a complainer and I provide her with a daily reason.

~~~

A man and wife were in divorce court, arguing over the custody of their children. The mother told the judge that since she brought the children into this world, she should retain custody. The man also wanted custody of his children, so the judge asked for his justification.

After a long silence, the man replied, "Your Honor, when I put a dollar in a vending machine and a Coke comes out, does the Coke belong to me or to the machine?"

~~~

A woman wakes up in the middle of the night and hears her husband crying like a baby. "What's wrong?" she asks.

"Honey, remember how twenty years ago I got you pregnant? And your dad said if I didn't marry you, he'd have me thrown in jail?"

"Yes, of course, but why is that making you cry now?"

"Because I would have been released today."

~~~

Q: What's the definition of divorce?
A: The future tense of marriage.

Q: If first marriages are triumphs of imagination over intelligence, what are second marriages?
A: Triumphs of hope over experience.

Q: What is the only thing divorce proves?
A: Whose mother was right in the first place.

Q: Did you hear about the new "Divorce Barbie?"
A: It comes with all of Ken's stuff.

~~~

Two souls with but a single thought,
Two hearts that beat as one.

~~~

On a bitterly cold winter morning a husband and a wife in Dublin were listening to the radio during breakfast. They heard the announcer say, "We are going to have 8 to 10 inches of snow today. You must park your car on the even-numbered side of the street, so the snow ploughs can get through." So the good wife went out and moved her car.

A week later while they are eating breakfast, again the radio announcer said, "We are expecting 10 to 12 inches of snow today. You must park your car on the odd-numbered side of the street, so the snow ploughs can get through." The good wife went out and moved her car again.

The next week they are again having breakfast when the radio announcer says, "We are expecting 12 to 14 inches of snow today. You must park...." Then the electric power went off. The good wife was very upset, and with a worried look on her face said, "I don't know what to do. Which side of the street do I have to park on so the snow ploughs can get through?"

Then with the love and understanding in his voice that all men who are married to blondes exhibit, the husband replied, "Why don't you just leave the bloody car in the garage this time."

THAT'S WHEN THE FIGHT STARTED....

Saturday morning I got up early, quietly dressed, made my lunch, grabbed the dog, and slipped quietly into the garage. I hooked the boat up to the car and proceeded to back out into a torrential downpour. The wind was blowing 50 mph, so I pulled back into the garage, turned on the radio and discovered that the weather would be bad all day. I went back into the house, quietly undressed and slipped back into bed. I cuddled up to my wife's back, now with a different anticipation and whispered, "The weather out there is terrible."

My loving wife of 10 years replied, "Can you believe my stupid husband is out fishing in that?"

And that's when the fight started....

I asked my wife, "Where do you want to go for our anniversary?"

It warmed my heart to see her face melt in sweet appreciation, "Somewhere I haven't been in a long time!" she said.

So I suggested, "How about the kitchen?"

And that's when the fight started....

My wife and I were watching 'Who Wants To Be A Millionaire' while we were in bed. I turned to her and said, "Are you in the mood for some lovin' tonight?"

"No," she answered.

I then said, "Is that your final answer?"

She didn't even look at me this time, simply saying, "Yes."

So I said, "Then I'd like to phone a friend."

And that's when the fight started....

I took my wife to a restaurant. The waiter, for some reason, took my order first. "I'll have the strip steak, medium rare, please."

He said, "Aren't you worried about mad cow?"

"Nope!" I said, "She can order for herself."

And that's when the fight started....

A woman is standing totally naked, looking in the bedroom mirror. She is not happy with what she sees and says to her husband, "I feel horrible. I look old, fat and ugly. I really need you to pay me a compliment about myself."

The husband replies, "Your eyesight's damn near perfect."

And that's when the fight started....

I tried to talk my wife into buying a case of Budweiser beer for $24.95. Instead, she bought a jar of face cream for $17.95. I told her the beer would make her look better to me at night than the face cream.

And that's when the fight started....

My wife asked me if a certain dress made her backside look big. I told her not as much as the dress she wore yesterday.

And that's when the fight started....

A man and a woman were asleep like two innocent babies. Suddenly, at 3:00 in the morning, a loud noise came from outside. The woman, bewildered, jumped up from the bed and yelled at the man, "Oh my gosh...that must be my husband!"

So the man jumped out of the bed, scared and naked jumped out the window. He smashed himself on the ground, ran through a thorn bush and to his car as fast as he could go. A few minutes later he returned and went up to the bedroom and screamed at the woman, "I AM your husband!"

The woman yelled back, "Yeah, then why were you running?"

And that's when the fight started....

~~~

On their wedding night, the young bride approached her new husband and asked for $20 for their first lovemaking encounter.

In his highly aroused state, her husband readily agreed.

This scenario was repeated each time they made love, for more than 40 years, with him thinking that it was a cute way for her to afford new clothes and other incidentals that she needed.

Arriving home around noon one day, she was surprised to find her husband in a very drunken state.

During the next few minutes, he explained that his employer was going through a process of corporate downsizing, and he had been let go.

It was unlikely that, at the age of 59, he'd be able to find another position that paid anywhere near what he'd been earning, and therefore, they were financially ruined. Calmly, his wife handed him a bank book which showed more than forty years of steady deposits and interest totalling nearly $1 million. Then she showed him certificates of deposits issued by the bank which were worth over $2 million, and informed him that they were one of the largest depositors in the bank. She explained that for more than three decades she had 'charged' him for sex, these holdings had multiplied and these were the results of her savings and investments.

Faced with evidence of cash and investments worth over $3 million, her husband was so astounded he could barely speak, but finally he found his voice and blurted out, "If I'd had any idea what you were doing I would have given you all my business!"

And that's when the fight started....

ILLUSIONS

Are you looking at the inside or outside of this book?

Standing Eskimo or Indian head?

Duck or rabbit?

AFTER

BEFORE
DRINKING

How many faces?

Young or old?

Saxophone or a woman's
face?

INSULTS

WHEN INSULTS HAD CLASS

These gorgeous insults are from an era when cleverness with words was still valued, before the great portion of the English language got boiled down to 4-letter words, not to mention waving middle fingers.

The exchange between Churchill and Lady Astor: She said, "If you were my husband I'd give you poison," and he said, "If you were my wife, I'd drink it."

A member of Parliament to Disraeli: "Sir, you will either die on the gallows or of some unspeakable disease." "That depends, Sir," said Disraeli, "whether I embrace your policies or your mistress."

"He had delusions of adequacy." Walter Kerr

"He has all the virtues I dislike and none of the vices I admire." Winston Churchill

"A modest little person, with much to be modest about." Winston Churchill

"I have never killed a man, but I have read many obituaries with great pleasure." Clarence Darrow

"He has never been known to use a word that might send a reader to the dictionary." William Faulkner (about Ernest Hemingway)

"Poor Faulkner. Does he really think big emotions come from big words?" Ernest Hemingway (about William Faulkner)

"Thank you for sending me a copy of your book, I'll waste no time reading it." Moses Hadas

"He can compress the most words into the smallest idea of any man I know." Abraham Lincoln

~~~

Quips, Quotes, Zingers & One Liners
129

I dialed a number and got the following recording:

"I am not available right now, but thank you for caring enough to call. I am making some changes in my life. Please leave a message after the Beep. If I do not return your call, you are one of the changes."

~~~

If Lucky Louie was looking for a needle in a haystack, he'd find the needle and the farmer's daughter as well.

~~~

Cy the Cynic couldn't make ends meet as a contortionist, couldn't type as a secretary, wasn't sooted to be a chimney sweep, and could only get time and a fifth for overtime in a distillery.

~~~

He wasn't hired as a faith healer because he lacked 'hands-on' experience.

JUNK MAIL

Three little words that work!!

The three little words are "Hold On, Please…"

Saying this, while putting down your phone and walking off (instead of hanging up immediately) would make each telemarketing call so much more time consuming that boiler room sales would grind to a halt.

Then when you eventually hear the phone company's 'beep-beep-beep' tone, you know it's time to go back and hang up your handset, which has efficiently completed its task.

These three little words will help eliminate telephone soliciting.

Do you ever get those annoying phone calls with no one on the other end?

This is a telemarketing technique where a machine makes phone calls and records the time of day when a person answers the phone.

This technique is used to determine the best time of day for a 'real' sales person to call back and get someone at home.

What you can do after answering, if you notice there is no one there, is to immediately start hitting your # button on the phone six or seven times, as quickly as possible. This confuses the machine that dialed the call and it kicks your number out of their system. Gosh, what a shame not to have your name in their system any longer!!

Junk Mail Help

When you get 'ads' enclosed with your phone or utility bill, return these 'ads' with your payment. Let the sending companies throw their own junk mail away.

When you get those 'pre-approved' letters in the mail for everything from credit cards to 2nd mortgages and similar type junk, do not throw away the return envelope.

Most of these come with postage paid envelopes, right? It costs them more than the regular postage IF and when they receive them back.

It costs them nothing if you throw them away! The postage was around 50 cents before the last increase, and it is according to the weight. In that case, why not get rid of some of your other junk mail and put it in these cool little, postage-paid return envelopes.

Send an ad for your local chimney cleaner to American Express. Send a pizza coupon to Citibank. If you didn't get anything else that day, then just send them their blank application back!

If you want to remain anonymous, just make sure your name isn't on anything you send them.

You can even send the envelope back empty if you want to just keep them guessing! It still costs them postage.

The banks and credit card companies are currently getting a lot of their own junk back in the mail, but folks, we need to OVERWHELM them. Let's let them know what it's like to get lots of junk mail and best of all they're paying for it…twice!

Let's help keep our postal service busy since they are saying that email is cutting into their business profits, and that's why they need to increase postage costs again. You get the idea! If enough people follow these tips, it will work. I have been doing this for years and I get very little junk mail anymore.

LANGUAGE

CLEVER WORDS FOR CLEVER PEOPLE

Arbitrator – a cook that leaves Arby's to work at McDonald's

Bernadette – the act of torching a mortgage

Burglarize – what a crook sees through

Avoidable – what a bullfighter tries to do

Eyedropper – clumsy ophthalmologist

Control – a short, ugly inmate

Counterfeiter – workers who put together kitchen cabinets

Eclipse – what an English barber does for a living

Left Bank – what the bank robbers did when their bag was full of money

Heroes – what a man in a boat does

Parasites – what you see from the Eiffel Tower

Paradox – two physicians

Pharmacist – a helper on a farm

Polarize – what penguins see through

Primate – remove your spouse from in front of TV

Relief – what trees do in the spring

Rubberneck – what you do to relax your wife

Selfish – what the owner of a seafood store does

Sudafed – Brought litigation against a government official

Paradigms – 20 cents

Quips, Quotes, Zingers & One Liners
137

Vegetarian – an old Indian word meaning 'poor hunter'. The politically correct version for 'poor hunter' is 'bow & arrow challenged'.

~~~

"Lexophile" is a word used to describe those that love using words in rather unique ways, such as 'you can tune a piano, but you can't tuna fish' or 'to write with a broken pencil is pointless.' A competition to see who can come up with the best one is held every year. This year's winning submission is posted at the very end.

- When fish are in schools, they sometimes take debate.
- A thief who stole a calendar got twelve months.
- When the smog lifts in Los Angeles U.C.L.A.
- The batteries were given out free of charge.
- A dentist and a manicurist married. They fought tooth and nail.
- A will is a dead giveaway.
- With her marriage, she got a new name and a dress.
- A boiled egg is hard to beat.
- When you've seen one shopping centre, you've seen a mall.
- Police were called to a daycare centre where a three year old was resisting a rest.
- Did you hear about the fellow whose whole left side was cut off? He's all right now.
- A bicycle can't stand alone; it is two tired.
- When a clock is hungry it goes back four seconds.
- The guy who fell onto an upholstery machine is now fully recovered.
- He had a photographic memory which was never developed.
- When she saw her first strands of gray hair she thought she'd dye.
- Acupuncture is a jab well done. That's the point of it.

And the cream of the wretched crop:

- Those who get too big for their pants will be exposed in the end.

~~~

A canner exceedingly canny,
One day remarked to his Granny,
A canner can can,
Anything that he can,
But he can't can a can, can he?

~~~

Last month, a worldwide telephone survey was conducted by the UN. The only question was, "Would you please give your honest opinion about possible solutions to the food shortage in the rest of the world?"

The survey was a complete failure because:

- In Eastern Europe they didn't know what 'honest' meant.
- In Western Europe they didn't know what 'shortage' meant.
- In Africa they didn't know what 'food' meant.
- In China they didn't know what 'opinion' meant.
- In the Middle East they didn't know what 'solution' meant.
- In South America they didn't know what 'please' meant.
- In the USA they didn't know what 'the rest of the world' meant.
- And in Britain everyone hung up as soon as they heard the Indian accent.

~~~

You think English is easy???

- The bandage was **wound** around the **wound**.
- The farm was used to **produce produce**.
- The dump was so full that it had to **refuse** more **refuse**.
- We must **polish** the **Polish** furniture.
- He could **lead** if he would get the **lead** out.
- The soldier decided to **desert** his dessert in the **desert**.

Quips, Quotes, Zingers & One Liners

- Since there is no time like the **present**, he thought it was time to **present** the **present**.
- A **bass** was painted on the head of the **bass** drum.
- When shot at, the **dove dove** into the bushes.
- I did not **object** to the **object**.
- The insurance was **invalid** for the **invalid**.
- There was a **row** among the oarsmen about how to **row**.
- They were too **close** to the door to **close** it.
- The buck **does** funny things when the **does** are present.
- A seamstress and a **sewer** fell down into a **sewer** line.
- To help with planting, the farmer taught his **sow** to **sow**.
- The **wind** was too strong to **wind** the sail.
- Upon seeing the **tear** in the painting I shed a **tear**.
- I had to **subject** the **subject** to a series of tests.
- How can I **intimate** this to my most **intimate** friend?
- When the actor took a **bow**, his **bow** fell off.
- I wanted to **live** by the ocean so I could see **live** whales.

Let's face it, English is a crazy language. There is no egg in eggplant, nor ham in hamburger, neither apple or pine in pineapple. English muffins weren't invented in England or French fries in France. Sweetmeats are candies while sweetbreads, which aren't sweet, are meat. We take English for granted. But if we explore its paradoxes, we find that quicksand can work slowly, boxing rings are square and a guinea big is neither from Guinea nor is it a pig.

And why is it that writers write but fingers don't fing, grocers don't groce and hammers don't ham? If the plural of tooth is teeth, why isn't the plural of booth, beeth? You have one goose, two geese, so one moose, two meese? One index, two indices?

Doesn't it seem crazy that you can make amends but not one amend? If you have a bunch of odds and ends and get rid of all but one of them, what do you call it?

If teachers taught, why didn't preachers praught? If a vegetarian eats vegetables, what does a humanitarian eat?

Sometimes I think all the English speakers should be committed to an asylum for the verbally insane. In what language do people recite at a play and play at a recital? Ship by truck and send cargo by ship? Have noses that run and feet that smell?

How can a slim chance and a fat chance be the same, while a wise man and a wise guy are opposites? You have to marvel at the unique lunacy of a language in which your house can burn up as it burns down, in which you fill in a form by filling it out, and in which an alarm goes off by going on.

English was invented by people, not computers, and it reflects the creativity of the human race, which of course, is not a race at all. That is why when the stars are out, they are visible, but when the lights are out, they are invisible.

PS – why doesn't 'Buick' rhyme with 'quick'?

~~~

To the citizens of the United States of America from Her Sovereign Majesty Queen Elizabeth II

In light of your failure in recent years to nominate competent candidates for President of the USA and thus to govern yourselves, we hereby give notice of the revocation of your independence, effective immediately. (You should look up 'revocation' in the Oxford English Dictionary.)

Her Sovereign Majesty Queen Elizabeth II will resume monarchial duties over all states, commonwealths and territories (except North Dakota, which she does not fancy.)

Your new Prime Minister, David Cameron, will appoint a Governor for America without the need for further elections.

Congress and the Senate will be disbanded. A questionnaire may be circulated next year to determine whether any of you noticed.

To aid in the transition to a British Crown dependency, the following rules are introduced with immediate effect:

1) The letter 'U' will be reinstated in words such as 'colour', 'favour', 'labour' and 'neighbour.' Likewise, you will learn to spell 'doughnut' without skipping half the letters, and the suffix '-ize' will be replaced by the suffix '-ise.' Generally, you will be expected to raise your vocabulary to acceptable levels. (Look up 'vocabulary')

2) Using the same twenty-seven words interspersed with filler noises such as 'like' and 'you know' is an unacceptable and inefficient form of communication. There is no such thing as U.S. English. We will let Microsoft know on your behalf. The Microsoft spell-checker will be adjusted to take into account the reinstated letter 'U' and the termination of '-ize.'

3) July 4th will no longer be celebrated as a holiday.

4) You will learn to resolve personal issues without using guns, lawyers, or therapists. The fact that you need so many lawyers and therapists shows that you're not quite ready to be independent. Guns should only be used for shooting grouse. If you can't sort things out without suing someone or speaking to a therapist, then you're not ready to shoot grouse.

5) Therefore, you will no longer be allowed to own or carry anything more dangerous than a vegetable peeler. Although a permit will be required if you wish to carry a vegetable peeler in public.

6) All intersections will be replaced with roundabouts, and you will start driving on the left side with immediate effect. At the same time, you will go metric with immediate effect and without the benefit of conversion tables. Both roundabouts and metrication will help you understand the British sense of humour.

7) The former USA will adopt UK prices on petrol (which you have been calling gasoline) of roughly $10/US gallon. Get used to it.

8) You will learn to make real chips. Those things you call French fries are not real chips, and those things you insist on calling potato chips are properly called crisps. Real chips are thick cut, fried in animal fat, and dressed not with catsup but with vinegar.

9) The cold, tasteless stuff you insist on calling beer is not actually beer at all. Henceforth, only proper British Bitter will be referred to as

beer, and European brews of known and accepted provenance will be referred to as Lager. South African beer is also acceptable, as they are pound for pound the greatest sporting nation on earth and it can only be due to the beer. They are also part of the British Commonwealth – see what it did for them! American brands will be referred to as Near-Frozen Gnat's Urine, so that all can be sold without risk of further confusion.

10) Hollywood will be required occasionally to cast English actors as good guys. Hollywood will also be required to cast English actors to play English characters. Watching Andie Macdowell attempt English dialect in Four Weddings and a Funeral was an experience akin to having one's ears removed with a cheese grater.

11) You will cease playing American football. There is only one kind of proper football, you call it soccer. Those of you brave enough will, in time, be allowed to play rugby (which has some similarities to American football, but does not involve stopping for a rest every twenty seconds or wearing full Kevlar body armour like a bunch of nannies).

12) Further, you will stop playing baseball. It is not reasonable to host an event called the World Series for a game which is not played outside of America. Since only 2.1% of you are aware there is a world beyond your borders, your error is understandable. You will learn cricket, and we will let you face the South Africans first to take the sting out of their deliveries.

13) You must tell us who killed JFK. It's been driving us mad.

14) An internal revenue agency (i.e. tax collector) from Her Majesty's Government will be with you shortly to ensure the acquisition of all monies due (backdated to 1776).

15) Daily Tea Time begins promptly at 4 p.m. with proper cups, with saucers, and never mugs, with high quality biscuits (cookies) and cakes; plus strawberries (with cream) when in season.

God Save the Queen!

~~~

What's the difference between stress, tension and panic?
Stress is when wife is pregnant. *Tension* is when girlfriend is pregnant.
And P*anic* is when both are pregnant.

RULES OF GRAMMAR

- Don't use double negatives.

- It's important to use apostrophe's right.

- Watch out for irregular verbs which has cropped into our language.

- About sentence fragments.

- Each pronoun agrees with their antecedent.

- Dangling, you should be careful about participles.

- Verbs has to agree with their subjects.

- Don't abbrev.

- And, of course, there is that old one: Never use a preposition to end a sentence with. As Winston Churchill once put it, "This is something up with which I shall not put."

- Check to see if you any words out.

- In letters themes reports articles and stuff like that you use commas to keep a string of objects apart.

- Join clauses good, like a conjunction should.

- Don't use run on sentences you've got to punctuate.

- In my opinion, I think that an author, when he is writing, should not get the habit of making use of too many unnecessary words that he does not need.

- Last, but not least, lay off clichés.

PUNCTUATE

That that is is that
That is not is not
That's it is

Quips, Quotes, Zingers & One Liners
144

PROOFREADING IS A DYING ART THESE DAYS!

Proof reading is a dying art, wouldn't you say?

MAN KILLS SELF BEFORE SHOOTING WIFE AND DAUGHTER
This one I caught in the SGV Tribune the other day and called the Editorial Room and asked who wrote this. It took two or three readings before the editor realized that what he was reading was impossible! They put in a correction the next day.

COLD WAVE LINKED TO TEMPERATURE
Who would have thought!

ENFIELD (LONDON) COUPLE SLAIN: POLICE SUSPECT HOMICIDE
They may be on to something!

RED TAPE HOLDS UP NEW BRIDGES
You mean there's something stronger than duct tape?

MAN STRUCK BY LIGHTNING: FACES BATTERY CHARGE
He probably IS the battery charge!

NEW STUDY OF OBESITY LOOKS FOR LARGER TEST GROUPS
Weren't they fat enough?

ASTRONAUT TAKES BLAME FOR GAS IN SPACECRAFT
That's what he gets for eating those beans!

KIDS MAKE NUTRITIOUS SNACKS
Do they taste like chicken?

LOCAL HIGH SCHOOL DROPOUTS CUT IN HALF
Chainsaw Massacre all over again!

HOSPITALS ARE SUED BY 7 FOOT DOCTORS
Boy, are they tall!

JUVENILE COURT TO TRY SHOOTING DEFENDANT
See if that works any better than a fair trial!

WAR DIMS HOPE FOR PEACE
I can see where it might have that effect!

Quips, Quotes, Zingers & One Liners
145

IF STRIKE ISN'T SETTLE QUICKLY, IT MAY LAST AWHILE
Ya think?!

MINERS REFUSE TO WORK AFTER DEATH
'No-good-for-nothing' lazy so-and-so's! They must be UNION!

SOMETHING WENT WRONG IN JET CRASH, EXPERT SAYS
Really? Ya think?

POLICE BEGIN CAMPAIGN TO RUN DOWN JAYWALKERS
Now that's taking things a bit far!

PANDA MATING FAILS; VETERINARIAN TAKES OVER
What a guy!

TYPHOON RIPS THROUGH CEMETERY; HUNDREDS DEAD
Really?

~~~

LEXIPHILES: WHOEVER PUT THESE TOGETHER LOVES LANGUAGE

The professor discovered that her theory of earthquakes was on shaky ground.

If you don't pay your exorcist you can get repossessed.

Show me a piano falling down a mineshaft and I'll show you A-flat miner.

You are stuck with your debt if you can't budget it.

If you take a laptop computer for a run you could job your memory.

~~~

Professor: "Joe, name two pronouns."
Joe: "Who, me?"

~~~

Quips, Quotes, Zingers & One Liners

Cdnuolt blveiee taht I cluod aulaclty uesdnatnrd waht I was rdanieg. The phaonmneal pweor of the hmuan mnid, aoccdrnig to rscheearch at Cmabrigde Uinervtisy, it dseno't mtaetr in waht oerdr the ltteres in a wrod are, the olny iproamtnt tihng is taht the frsit and lsat ltteer be in the rghit pclae.

The rset can be a taotl mses and you can sitll raed it whotuit a pboerlm. Tihs is bcuseae the huamn mnid deos not raed ervey lteter by istlef, but the wrod as a wlohe. Azanmig huh?

A LEGEND

RED SKELTON'S RECIPE FOR THE PERFECT MARRIAGE

1) Two times a week we go to a nice restaurant, have a little beverage, good food and companionship. She goes on Tuesdays, I go on Fridays.

2) We also sleep in separate beds. Hers is in California and mine is in Texas.

3) I take my wife everywhere....but she keeps finding her way back.

4) I asked my wife where she wanted to go for our anniversary. 'Somewhere I haven't been in a long time!' she said. So I suggested the kitchen.

5) We always hold hands. If I let go, she shops.

6) She has an electric blender, electric toaster and electric bread maker. She said 'There are too many gadgets, and no place to sit down!' So I bought her an electric chair.

7) My wife told me the car wasn't running well because there was water in the carburetor. I asked where the car was. She told me, 'In the lake.'

8) She got a mud pack, and looked great for two days. Then the mud fell off.

9) She ran after the garbage truck, yelling, 'Am I too late for the garbage?' The driver said, 'No, jump in!'

10) Remember: Marriage is the number one cause of divorce.

11) I married Miss Right. I just didn't know her first name was Always.

12) I haven't spoken to my wife in 18 months. I don't like to interrupt her.

LIFE

WHAT YOU MIGHT HAVE HEARD SAID IN THE FIFTIES

I'll tell you one thing, if things keep going the way they are, it's going to be impossible to buy a week's groceries for $20.

Have you seen the new cars coming out next year? It won't be long when $3,000 will only buy a good used one.

If they think I am going to pay 50 cents for a hair cut, forget it. I'll have my wife learn to cut hair.

If a few idiots want to risk their necks flying across the country that's fine, but nothing will ever replace trains.

There's no sense going into the city anymore for a weekend, what with hotels charging $8.00 per room.

When I first started driving, who would have thought gas would some day cost 40 cents a gallon.

~~~

Money is the root of all evil. So I try to spend it before it corrupts me.

If a mother's place is in the home, why am I always in the car?

Seen it all, done it all, can't remember most of it.

If at first you don't succeed, try it your wife's way.

~~~

My wife said, "Watcha doin' today?"
I said, "Nothing."
She said, "You did that yesterday."
I said, "I wasn't finished."

~~~

A man who was a keen golfer phoned the doctor. "Doctor, come quick, this is an emergency! My young son has swallowed my golf tees!"

"Okay," said the doctor, "I'll be with you as soon as I can."

"Tell me what to do till you get here?"

The doctor said, "Practise your putting."

~~~

Did you hear about the couple who met in a revolving door? They're still going round together.

Sure marriage can be fun some of the time. Trouble is, you're married all of the time.

Did you hear about the man who read a book about anti-gravity? It was impossible to put down.

HE COULD DO ABSOLUTELY ANYTHING!

George walked out into the street and managed to get a taxi just going by. He got into the taxi and the cabbie says, "Perfect timing. You're just like Dave."

"Who?" says George.

"Dave Edwards. There's a guy who did everything right. For instance, like my coming along just when you needed a cab. It would have happened like that to Dave."

"There are always a few clouds over everybody," says George.

"Oh, not Dave," the cabbie responded, "He was a terrific athlete. He could have gone on the pro tour in tennis. He could golf with the pros. He sang like an opera baritone and danced like Fred Astair."

So George says, "He was something, huh?"

The cabbie continues, "He had a memory like a trap. Could remember everybody's birthday. He knew all about wine, which fork to eat with. He could fix anything – a real handyman. Not like me – I change a fuse and I black out the whole neighbourhood."

"A fellow like that, no wonder you remember him," George says.

"Well, I never actually met Dave," the cabby responds.

"Then how do you know so much about him?" George asks.

"Because....I married his widow."

DEFINITION OF MATURITY

Maturity is the ability to control anger and settle differences without violence or destruction.

Maturity is patience, the willingness to pass up immediate pleasure in favour of the long term gain.

Maturity is perseverance, the ability to sweat out a project or a situation in spite of opposition and discouraging setbacks.

Maturity is unselfishness – responding to the needs of others, often at the expense of one's own desire or wishes.

Maturity is the capacity to face unpleasantness and frustration, discomfort and defeat, without complaint or collapse.

Maturity is humility. It is being big enough to say, "I was wrong." And when right, the mature person need not say, "I told you so."

Maturity is the ability to make a decision and stand by it. The immature spend their lives exploring endless possibilities that do nothing.

Quips, Quotes, Zingers & One Liners
157

If life were fair, Elvis would be alive and all the impersonators would be dead.

Johnny Carson

Mona Lisa

Original   In U.S.A.

TURN YOUR STUMBLING BLOCKS INTO STEPPING STONES.

Silence is golden but duct tape is better.

The real art of conversation is not only to say the right thing at the right time, but also to leave unsaid the wrong thing at the tempting moment.

THE HUMOR OF STEVEN WRIGHT

If you're not familiar with the work of Steven Wright, he's the famous scientist who once said, "I woke up one morning and all my stuff had been stolen and replaced by exact duplicates." His mind sees things differently than we do, to our amazement and amusement. Here are some of his gems:

- I'd kill for a Nobel Peace Prize.
- Borrow money from pessimists – they don't expect it back.
- Half the people you know are below average.
- 99% of lawyers give the rest a bad name.
- 42.7% of all statistics are made up on the spot.
- A conscience is what hurts when all your other parts feel so good.
- The early bird may get the worm, but the second mouse gets the cheese.
- I almost had a psychic girlfriend but she left me before we met.
- Okay, so what's the speed of dark?
- How do you tell when you're out of invisible ink?
- If everything seems to be going well, you have obviously overlooked something.
- Depression is merely anger without enthusiasm.

Quips, Quotes, Zingers & One Liners

~~~

When everything is coming your way, you're in the wrong lane.

Ambition is a poor excuse for not having enough sense to be lazy.

Hard work pays off in the future, laziness pays off now.

I intend to live forever – so far, so good.

If Barbie is so popular, why do you have to buy her friends?

Eagles may soar, but weasels don't get sucked into jet engines.

What happens if you get scared half to death twice?

My mechanic told me, "I couldn't repair your brakes, so I made your horn louder."

Why do psychics have to ask you for your name?

If at first you don't succeed, destroy all evidence that you tried.

A conclusion is the place where you got tired of thinking.

Experience is something you don't get until just after you need it.

The hardness of the butter is proportional to the softness of the bread.

Success depends on your backbone, not your wishbone.

NINE REASONS WHY I DON'T EXERCISE

1) For every mile you jog, you add one minute to life. This enables you, at the age of 85 to add an additional five months in a nursing home at $5,000 per month.

2) My grandmother started walking five miles a day when she was 60. She's now 97 and we don't know where the hell she is.

3) I joined a health club last year and spent about $400. I haven't lost a pound. Apparently you have to show up.

4) I have to exercise in the morning before my brain figures out what I'm doing.

5) I don't exercise at all. If God meant me to touch my toes he'd have put them further up my body.

6) I like long walks especially when they are taken by people who annoy me.

7) The advantage of exercise every day is that you die healthier.

8) If you are going to try cross country skiing, start with a small country.

9) I don't jog. It makes the ice jump right out of my glass.

LIFE IS BACKWARDS

I think the life cycle is all backwards. You should start out dead and get it out of the way. Then, you wake up in an old age home feeling better every day. You get kicked out for being too healthy; go collect your pension, then when you start work, you get a gold watch on your first day. You work 40 years until you're young enough to enjoy your retirement. You drink alcohol, you party, you're generally promiscuous and you get ready for high school. You go to primary school, you become a kid, you play, you have no responsibilities, you become a baby, and then....

You'll spend your last nine months floating peacefully in luxury, in space-like conditions; central heating, room service on tap, larger quarters every day, and then, you finish off as a gleem in a father's eye.

~~~

Anything good in life is either illegal, immoral or fattening.

Be nice to your kids. They'll choose your nursing home.

Bigamy: one husband too many
Monogamy: same thing

Don't take life seriously, it's not permanent.

Exceptions always outnumber rules.

Few women admit their age. Few men act theirs.

Friendship is one soul in two bodies.

I don't suffer from insanity, I enjoy every moment of it.

Senility isn't so bad, you keep meeting new friends.

Women like quiet men, they think they are listening.

I used to have a handle on life, then it broke.

You can agree with me or you can be wrong.

I'm in shape, round is a shape.

My idea of exercise is a good brisk sit.

Here I am. Now what are you're other two wishes.

If only I was rich instead of beautiful.

My mind works like lightening. One brilliant flash and it's gone.

I don't procrastinate. I reschedule.

Forget love. I'd rather fall in chocolate.

There's nothing wrong with me that a little chocolate won't fix.

There's nothing better than a good friend, except a good friend with chocolate.

Funny, I don't remember being absent-minded.

So much chocolate, so little time!

I feel terrific since I've gone into denial.

Lord, if you won't make me skinny, please make my friends fat.

When in doubt, simply add more wine.

Good morning, let the stress begin.

The more people I meet, the more I like my dog.

The more people I meet, the more I like my cat.

Like good wine, I've aged to perfection.

~~~

If my body were a car, this is the time I would be thinking about trading it in for a newer model. I've got bumps and dents and scratches in my finish and my paint job is getting a little dull.

But that's not the worst of it. My headlights are out of focus and it's especially hard to see things up close. My traction is not as graceful as it once was. I slip and slide and skid and bump into things even in the best of weather. My whitewalls are stained with varicose veins. It takes me hours to reach my maximum speed. My fuel rate burns inefficiently.

But worst of it, almost every time I sneeze, cough or sputter, either my radiator leaks or my exhaust backfires!

PLANS

Today I'll dust my flute and play
A wondrous tune, and far away
A lark will know its meaning
I'll sing, and listeners far and near
Will marvel at the sound they hear
(But first I'll finish cleaning)

Today I'll take a piece of clay
And make a form that lives to say
That beauty is unending
I'll paint a picture that when shown
Art connoisseurs will fight to own
(When I've done the mending)

Today I'll let the tide in me
Swell forth the things inside of me,
At least by afternoon

I'll do the things I ache to do
I'll find the time they take to do
Well not today – but soon.

GENTLE THOUGHTS FOR THE DAY

One of the many things no one tells you about aging is that it is such a nice change from being young.

A penny saved is a government oversight.

Birds of a feather flock together and crap on your car.

When I'm feeling down, I like to whistle. It makes the neighbour's dog run to the end of his chain and gag himself.

The older you get, the tougher it is to lose weight because by then your body and your fat have gotten to be really good friends.

~~~

When faced with a decision – decide.
When faced with a choice – choose.
Sitting on the fence will leave you too tense
Because you neither win nor lose!
Barry Spilchuk

You live longer once you realize that any time spent being unhappy is wasted.
Ruth E. Renkl

You may be disappointed if you fail, but you are doomed if you don't try.
Beverly Sills

The measure of a man's real character is what he would do if he knew he would never be found out.
T.B. Macaulay

A happy person is not a person in a certain set of circumstances, but rather a person with a certain set of attitudes.
Hugh Downs

~~~

LIFE.*

*Available for a limited time only. Limit one (1) per person. Subject to change without notice. Provided "as is" and without any warranties. Non-transferable and is the sole responsibility of the recipient. May incur damages arising from use or misuse. Additional parts sold separately. Your mileage may vary. Subject to all applicable fees and taxes. Terms and conditions apply. Other restrictions apply.

THREE SIMPLE RULES IN LIFE.

1. If you do not GO after what you want, you'll never have it.

2. If you do not ASK, the answer will always be NO.

3. If you do not step forward, you'll always be in the same place.

In the end, we only regret the chances we didn't take, relationships we are afraid to have, and the decisions we waited too long to make.

Someday, everything will make perfect sense. So, for now, laugh at the confusion, smile through the tears and keep reminding yourself that everything happens for a reason.

Slow down and enjoy the journey right now. Take time for the people in your life. They won't always be there.

YOUR VALUE DOESN'T DECREASE BASED ON SOMEONE'S INABILITY TO SEE YOUR WORTH.

If there are no ups and downs in your life, it means you are dead.

You never appreciate what you have till it's gone. Toilet paper is a good example.

One of the best feelings in the world is knowing that your presence and absence both mean something to someone.

It's your road and yours alone, others may walk it with you, but no one can walk it for you.

IN THE PRICE OF GREATNESS IS RESPONSIBILITY.

Give a man a fish and he will eat for a day. Teach a man to fish and he will sit in a boat all day drinking beer.

When you go into court, you are putting yourself in the hands of twelve people, who weren't smart enough to get out of jury duty.

MARRIAGE

I MADE A WISH AND YOU CAME TRUE.

IF I COULD CHOOSE AGAIN, I'D STILL CHOOSE YOU.

ONE WAY FOR A GIRL TO STOP A MAN MAKING LOVE TO HER IS TO MARRY HIM.

Making marriage work is like working on a farm. You have to start again each morning.

ROMANCE IS LIKE CHESS. ONE FALSE MOVE AND YOU'RE MATED.

A wedding is where a man loses complete control of himself.

MEDICAL

A doctor says to her patient, "I've got good news and bad news. Which do you want first?"

The patient says, "Give me the bad news first."

The doctor replies, "Okay, the bad news is, you have brain cancer."

"What?! That's awful news, doc. What about the good news?"

"You've also got Alzheimer's disease," the doctor replies.

The patient looks relieved and says, "Oh, that's not so bad. At lease I don't have brain cancer."

~~~

Q: What did the nurse say when she found a rectal thermometer in her pocket?
A: "Some ---hole has my pen."

~~~

Two nurses overheard a doctor yelling, "Tetanus! Measles! Polio!"

"Why is that doctor yelling?" one nurse asked another nurse.

She replied, "He just likes to call the shots around here."

~~~

A distaught older woman called her doctor. "Is it true," she asked, "that the medication you prescribed has to be taken for the rest of my life?"

"Yes, I'm afraid so," the doctor told her.

There was a moment of silence before the woman asked, "I'm wondering, then, just how serious is my condition? This prescription is marked 'No Refills.'"

~~~

Patient: Doctor, my wife is going through menopause. What can I do?

Doctor: Finish your bsement if you're handy with tools. When you're done you'll have a place to live.

~~~

Grampa recently turned sixty-five and went to the doctor for a complete physical. After an exam the doctor said grandpa was doing 'fairly well' for his age. Grandpa was a little concerned and asked, "Doc, do you think I'll live to eighty?"

The doctor asked, "Do you smoke tobacco or drink alcohol?"

"Oh no," Grandpa replied, "and I don't' do drugs, either."

"Do you have many friends and entertain frequently?"

Grandpa said, "No, I usually stay home and keep to myself."

"Do you eat beef and pork?"

"No, my other doctor said red meat is unhealthy!"

"Do you spend a lot of time doing things in the sun, like playing golf, sailing, or bicycling?"

"No, I don't."

"Do you gamble, drive fast cars, or have lots of sex?"

"No, I don't do any of those things anymore."

The doctor looked at Grandpa and said, "Then why do you care?"

~~~

An artist asked the gallery owner if there had been any interest in his paintings currently on display. "I've got good news and bad news," the owner replied. "The good news is that a gentleman inquired about your work and wondered if it would appreciate in value after your death. When I told him it would, he bought all ten of your paintings."

"That's great! What's the bad new?"

The gallery owner replied, "The guy was your doctor."

~~~

Patient: Doctor, is it common for sixty-four year olds to have problems with short-term membory storage?

Doctor: The problem is not storing memory. The problem is retrieval.

~~~

An old man went to his doctor for a routine checkup. The doctor asked him about his sex life.

"Well," the old man said, "it's not bad at all, to be honest. My wife ain't all that interested anymore, so I just cruise around looking for action. In the past week I had sex with total strangers in a park."

"At your age!" the doctor said. "I hope you had a least take some precautions."

"Doc, I may be old but I ain't stupid!" the man said, "I gave 'em all a phoney name."

~~~

A ninety-year-old man is having his annual checkup. The doctor asks him how he's doing.

"I've never been better!" the old man replies. "I have an eighteen-year-old bride who is pregnant with my child! What do you think about that?"

The doctor considers this for a moment and says, "I know a guy who is an avid hunter. He never misses a season. But one day, he is in a hurry and he accidentally grabs his umbrella instead of his gun. So he walks in the woods and spots a deer hiding in the brush. He raises his umbrella, points it at the deer and squeezes the handle. BANG! The deer drops dead in front of him."

"That's impossible!" the old man says, "Somebody else must have shot that deer."

The doctor nods in agreement, "Exactly."

DOCTOR, DOCTOR!

Patient: Doctor, doctor! I feel like a pack of cards.
Doctor: I'll deal with you later.

Patient: Doctor, doctor! Can I get a second opinion?
Doctor: Of course, come back tomorrow.

Patient: Doctor, doctor! I think I'm a bridge.
Doctor: What's come over you?

Patient: Doctor, doctor! I keep thinking I'm a set of curtains.
Doctor: Pull yourself together,man.

Patient: Doctor, doctor! You have to help me out.
Doctor: Certianly, which way did you come in?

Patient: Doctor, doctor! I've broken my arm in two places.
Doctor: So don't go back to those two places.

Patient: Doctor, doctor! I feel like a small bucket.
Doctor: You do look a little pale.

Patient: Doctor, doctor! I feel like a spoon.
Doctor: Sit still and don't stir.

Patient: Doctor, doctor! I think I'm a wood worm.
Doctor: How boring for you.

Patient: Doctor, doctor! I've got a strawberry growing out of my head.
Doctor: I'll give you some cream to put on it.

~~~

The doctor said that I should have come in earlier. I said, "I did but I've been in the waiting room for three hours."

~~~

A man contacted his Acupunturist about a headache. She said, "It's late, take two tacks and call me in the morning."

Quips, Quotes, Zingers & One Liners

MORAL OF THE STORY

An eagle was sitting on a tree resting, doing nothing. A small rabbit saw the eagle and asked him, "Can I also sit like you and do nothing?"

The eagle answered, "Sure, why not."

So, the rabbit sat on the ground below the eagle and rested. All of a sudden, a fox appeared, jumped on the rabbit and ate it.

Moral of the story: To be sitting and doing nothing, you must be sitting very high up.

~~~

OLD AGE

Another two elderly people living in The Villages, he a widower and she a widow, had known each other for a number of years. One evening there was a neighborhood supper in the local rec center.

The two were at the same table, across from one another. As the meal went on, he took a few admiring glances at her, and finally gathered the courage to ask her, "Will you marry me?"

After about six seconds of 'careful consideration', she answered, "Yes. Yes, I will."

The meal ended and, with a few more pleasant exchanges, they went to their respective places. Next morning, he was troubled. "Did she say 'yes' or did she say 'no'?"

He couldn't remember. Try as he might, he just could not recall. Not even a faint memory. With trepidation, he went to the telephone and called her. First, he explained that he didn't remember as well as he used to. Then he reviewed the lovely evening past. As he gained a little more courage, he inquired, "When I asked if you would marry me, did you say yes or no?"

He was delighted to hear her say, "Why, I said yes, yes I will, and I meant it with all my heart." Then she continued, "I am so glad that you called because I couldn't remember who had asked me."

~~~

A doctor was addressing a large audience in Tampa, "The material we put into our stomachs is enough to have killed most of us sitting here years ago; red meat is awful; soft drinks corrode your stomach lining; Chinese food is loaded with MSG; high fat diets can be disastrous, and none of us realizes the long-term harm caused by the germs in our drinking water. However, there is one thing that is the most dangerous of all and we have eaten it, or will eat it. Can anyone here tell me what food it is that causes the most grief and suffering for us?"

After several seconds of quiet, a 75-year-old man in the front row raised his hand, and softly said, "Wedding Cake?"

~~~

One night an 87-year-old woman came home from Bingo to find her 92-year-old husband in bed with another woman. She became violent and ended up pushing him off the balcony of their 20th floor apartment, killing him instantly.

Brought before the court, on the charge of murder, she was asked if she had anything to say in her own defense.

"Your Honor," she began cooly, "I figured that at 92, if he could screw, he could fly."

~~~

Bob, a 70-year-old, extremely wealthy widower shows up at the Country Club with a breathtakingly beautiful and very sexy 25-year-old blonde-haired woman who knocks everyone's socks off with her youthful sex appeal and charm and who hangs over Bob's arm and listens to his every word. His buddies at the club are all aghast.

At the very first chance, they corner him and ask, "Bob, how'd you get the trophy girlfriend?"

Bob replies, "Girlfriend? She's my wife!"

They are knocked over, but continue to ask, "So how'd you persuade her to marry you?"

"I lied about my age," Bob replies.

"What, did you tell her you were only 50?"

Bob smiles ands says, "No, I told her I was 90."

~~~

A group of Americans were traveling by tour bus through Holland. As they stopped at a cheese farm, a young guide led them through the process of cheese making, explaining that goat's milk was used. She showed the group a lovely hillside where many goats were grazing. "These," she explained, "are the older goats put out to pasture when they no longer produce."

She then asked, "What do you do in America with your old goats?" and a spry old gentleman answered, "They send us on bus tours!"

~~~

Designers have invented a new bra for middle-aged women.
They've call it The Sheepdog, as it rounds them up and points them in the right direction.

~~~

Reporters interviewing a 104-year-old woman, "And what do you think is the best thing about being 104?" the reporter asked.

She simply replied, "No peer pressure."

~~~

Just before the funeral services, the undertaker came up to the very elderly widow and asked, "How old was your husband?"

"98," she replied. "Two years younger than me."

"So you're 100," the undertaker commented.

She responded, "Hardly worth going home, is it?"

~~~

I've sure gotten old. I've had two by-pass surgeries, a hip replacement, new knees, fought prostate cancer, and diabetes.

I'm half blind, can't hear anything quieter than a jet engine, take 40 different medications that make me dizzy, winded, and subject to blackouts.

I have bouts with dementia, poor circulation, hardly feel my hands and feet anymore. Can't remember if I'm 85 or 92. Have lost all my friends. But.....thank God, I still have my Florida driver's license.

~~~

God, grant me the senility
To forget the people
I never liked anyway,
The good fortune
To run into the ones I do,
And the eyesight to tell the difference.

~~~

Sometimes I laugh so hard the tears run down my leg.

I smile because I don't know what the hell is going on.

I'm ready for a great day. I've got my coffee and cigarettes and I've had a Prozac.

Sometimes everything seems quite clear and then I regain consciousness.

Grow old with me. You ain't seen nothing yet.

Don't let aging get you down. It's too hard to get up again.

Your mind may wander, but mine leaves completely.

Living in a small town has one big advantage. If you forget what you are doing, someone can tell you.

Multi-tasking comes with age. I can laugh, sneeze and pee at the same time.

I don't have an attitude. I have a personality which you can't handle.

OLD IS...
...NOT CARING WHERE YOUR SPOUSE GOES.
...THE DOCTOR, NOT THE POLICE, TELLING YOU TO SLOW DOWN.
...NOT HAVING TO TAKE A LAXATIVE WHEN YOU GET A LITTLE ACTION.
...FEELING YOUNGER THAN OTHERS LOOK AT A CLASS REUNION.

A senior citizen said to his eighty-year-old buddy, "So, I hear you're getting married?"
"Yep!"
"Do I know her?"
"Nope!"
"This woman, is good looking?"
"Not really."
"Is she a good cook?"

"Naw, she can't cook too well."
"Does she have lots of money?"
"Nope! Poor as a church mouse."
"Well, then, is she good in bed?"
"I don't know."
"Why in the world do you want to marry her then?"
"Because she can still drive!"

~~

Three old guys are out walking. The first one says, "Windy, isn't it?"
The second one says, "No, it's Thursday."
The third one says, "So am I, let's go grab a beer."

~~~

Forget health food,
I'm at an age where I need all the preservatives I can get.

~~~

Frustration is trying to find your glasses without your glasses.

~~~

The irony of life is that, by the time you're old enough to know your way
around, you're not going anywhere.

~~~

I was always taught to respect my elders,
but it keeps getting harder to find one.

~~~

Do you realize that in about 40 years, we'll have thousands of old ladies
running around with tattoos? And rap music will be the Golden Oldies!

~~~

Old age doesn't begin at 40, but gravity does.

~~~

Old is…when 'getting lucky' means you find your car in the parking lot.
Old is…when an 'all nighter' means not getting up to use the bathroom.
Old is…when you're not sure if these are facts or jokes…

~~~

Please give my rocking chair a push.

Why did I go all those years resisting temptation?

I read the obits each day to see if my name is there.

I get winded playing dominoes.

I'm having an affair but I can't remember with whom.

I must need glasses, my children are beginning to look middle-aged.

~~~

GOTTA KEEP THE OLD MOTOR RUNNING

The marriage of an 80-year-old man and a 20-year-old woman was the talk of the town. After being married a year, the couple went to the hospital for the birth of their first child.

The attending nurse came out of the delivery room to congratulate the old gentleman and said, "This is amazing. How do you do it at your age?"

The old man grinned and said, "You got to keep the old motor running."

The following year, the couple returned to the hospital for the birth of their second child. The same nurse was attending the delivery and again went out to congratulate the old gentleman. She said, "Sir, you are something else. How do you manage it?"

The old man grinned and said, "You gotta keep the old motor running."

A year later, the couple returned to the hospital for the birth of their third child. The same nurse was there for this birth and, after the delivery, she once again approached the old gentleman, smiled, and said, "Well, you surely are something else! How do you do it?"

The old man replied, "It's like I've told you before, you gotta keep the old motor running."

The nurse, still smiling, patted him on the back and said, "Well, I guess it's time to change the oil. This one's black."

~~~

Wrinkled was not one of the things I wanted to be when I grew up.

Consciousness – that annoying time between naps.

Being 'over the hill' is much better than being under it!

I have reached the age where 'happy hour' is a nap.

~~~

SKINNY DIPPIN'

An elderly man in Florida had owned a large farm for several years. He had a large pond in the back, fixed up nice picnic tables, horseshoe pits, and some orange and grapefruit trees. The pond was properly shaped and fixed up for swimming when it was built.

One evening the old farmer decided to go down to the pond to look it over, as he hadn't been there for a while. He grabbed a five-gallon bucket to bring back some fruit.

As he neared the pond, he heard voices shouting and laughing with glee. As he came closer, he saw it was a bunch of young women skinny-dipping in his pond. He made the women aware of his presence and they all went to the deep end.

One of the women shouted to him, "We're not coming out until you leave!"

The old man frowned, "I didn't come down here to watch you ladies swim naked or make you get out of the pond naked." Holding the bucket up he said, "I'm here to feed the alligator."

Old men can think fast...

GOODBYE, MOM

A young man shopping in a supermarket noticed a little old lady following him around. If he stopped, she stopped. Furthermore, she kept staring at him. She finally overtook him at the checkout. She turned to him and said, "I hope I haven't made you feel ill at ease; it's just that you look so much like my late son."

He answered, "That's okay."

"I know it's silly, but if you'd call out 'goodbye, Mom" as I leave the store, it would make me feel so happy."

She then went through the checkout. As she was on her way out of the store, the man called out, "Goodbye, Mom."

The little old lady waved, and smiled back at him. Pleased that he had brought a little sunshine into someone's day, he went to pay for his groceries.

"That comes to $121.85," said the clerk.

"How come so much? I only bought five items!"

The clerk replied, "Yeah, but your mother said you'd be paying for her things, too."

~~~

Two elderly gentlemen from a retirement center were sitting on a bench under a tree when one turns to the other and says, "Slim, I'm 83-years-old now and I'm just full of aches and pains. I know you're about my age. How do you feel?"

Slim says, "I feel just like a newborn baby today."

"Really?! Like a newborn baby?!"

"Yep, no hair, no teeth, and I think I just wet my pants."

~~~

An elderly couple had dinner at another couple's house, and after eating, the wives left the table and went into the kitchen.

The two gentlemen were talking, and one said, "Last night we went out to a new restaurant and it was really great. I would recommend it very highly."

The other man said, "What is the name of the restaurant?"

The first man thought and finally said, "What is the name of that flower you give to someone you love? You know…the one that's red and has thorns."

"Do you mean a rose?"

"Yes, that's the one," replied the man. He then turned towards the kitchen and yelled, "Rose, what's the name of that restaurant we went to last night?"

~~~

Have you ever been guilty of looking at others your own age and thinking, "Surely, I can't look that old?" Well….you'll love this one!

I was sitting in the waiting room for my first appointment with a new dentist. I noticed his DDS diploma, which bore his full name. Suddenly, I remembered a tall, handsome, dark-haired boy with the same name had been in my high school class some 40-odd years ago. Could he be the same guy that I had a secret crush on, way back when? Upon seeing him, however, I quickly discarded any such thought. This balding, gray-haired man with the deeply lined face was way too old to have been my classmate. Hmmm…or could he???

After he examined my teeth, I asked him if he had attended Morgan Park High School. "Yes, I did. I'm a Mustang," he gleamed with pride."

"When did you graduate?" I asked.

He answered, "In 1959. Why do you ask?"

"You were in my class!" I exclaimed. He looked at me closely. Then, that ugly, old, wrinkled son-of-a-bitch asked, "What did you teach?"

For Those Born Before 1945

We were born before television, before penicillin, before polio shots, frozen foods, Xerox, plastic, contact lenses and the Pill. We were born before radar, credit cards, split atoms, laser beams and ball point pens. Before pantyhose, clothes dryers, electric blankets, air conditioning, drip-dry clothes...and before man walked on the moon.

We got married first and then lived together. How quaint can you be? In our time closets were for clothes, not 'coming out of'. Bunnies were small rabbits and rabbits were not Volkswagons. Designer jeans were scheming girls named Jean and having a meaningful relationship meant getting along with our cousins.

We thought fast-food was what you ate during Lent and outerspace was the back row of the movie theatre. We were before house husbands, gay rights, computer dating, dual careers and commuter marriages. We were before daycare centres, group therapy and nursing homes. We never heard of FM radio, tape decks, electronic typewriters, word processors, artificial hearts, yogurt and guys wearing earrings. For us, time sharing meant togetherness, not computers and condominiums. A chip meant a piece of wood. Hardware meant hardware and software wasn't even a word.

Back then 'Made in Japan' meant junk and the term 'making out' referred to how you did in your exam. Pizzas, McDonalds and instant coffee were unheard of. We hit the scene where there were 5 and 10 cent stores, where you bought things for 5 and 10 cents. Stores sold ice cream cones for a nickel or a dime. For one nickel you could ride a street car, make a phone call, buy a Pepsi or enough stamps to mail one letter *and* two postcards. You could buy a new Chevy coupe for $600...but who could afford one? A pity too, because gas was only 11 cents a gallon.

In our day, grass was mowed, coke was a cold drink and pot was something you cooked in. Rock music was a Grandma's lullaby and Aids were helpers in the principal's office. We were certainly not before the differences between the sexes were discovered, but we were surely before the sex change. We made do with what we had. And we were the last generation that was so dumb as to think you needed a husband to have a baby.

No wonder we're so confused and there is such a generation gap today. But we survived! What better reason to celebrate.

~~~

When you don't wear somethng for a while, it shrinks.

Time moves so quickly that tomorrow comes along just as you are getting accustomed to today.

~~~

An older gentleman was on the operating table awaiting surgery and he insisted that his son, a renowned surgeon, perform the operation. As he was about to get the anesthesia he asked to speak to his son.

"Yes Dad, what is it?"

"Don't be nervous son; do your best and just remember, if it doesn't go well, if something happens to me, your mother is going to come and live with you and your wife..."

~~~

The older we get, the fewer things seem worth waiting in line for.

Age brings wisdom or age shows up alone. You never know.

All my favorate memories are in the past.

If you think pushing 60 is hard, wait until you start dragging it.

Life is short, break the rules.

It's not the dying that bothers me, it's the not being here anymore.

I'm not deaf. I'm ignoring you.

You can keep your stomach in for just so many years.

If you think there's good in everybody, you haven't met everybody.

I intend to live forever. So far so good.

Happy hour is a nap.

Now that I'm old, I've become a valuable antique.

Hair of silver, teeth of gold and joints of lead.

There's always a lot to be thankful for if you take time to look for it. For example, I am sitting here thinking now nice it is that wrinkles don't hurt.

After a certain age, if you don't wake up aching somewhere, you may be dead.

The only two things we do with greater frequency at our age are urinate and attend funerals.

Try not to let your mind wander. It is too small and fragile to be out alone.

I know some of you are not old enough to get this!

Old is when...your sweetie says, "Let's go upstairs and make love," and you answer, "Pick one, I can't do both!"

Old is when...your friends compliment you on your new alligator shoes and you're barefoot.

Old is when...going braless pulls all the wrinkles out of your face.

A SMILE FOR TODAY

Mrs. Walinski says:

Have you noticed that everything is farther away than it used to be? It is twice as far to the corner and I've noticed they've added a hill. I've given up running for the bus. It leaves faster than it used to. It seems they are making stairs steeper than in the old days, and have you noticed the small print they now use in the newspapers? There is no use asking anyone to read aloud, everyone speaks in such a low voice I can hardly hear them.

The material in clothes is so skimpy now, especially around the waist. It is almost impossible to reach my shoelaces and I cannot figure out why. Even people are changing. They are so much younger than they used to be when I was their age and on the other hand, people my own age are so much older than I am. I ran across a classmate the other day and she had aged so much, she didn't know me. I got to thinking about the poor thing while I was combing my hair this morning and in doing so, I glanced at my reflection. Really now, they just don't make a good mirror anymore.

The other day I was asked if I got lonesome living alone. Why I don't live alone! I live with four men. I get up with Charlie Horse, I have lunch with Arth Ritis, spend the day with Will Power and go to bed with Ben Gay.

~~~

Senior citizens are the nation's leading carriers of AIDS! Hearing AIDS, Band AIDS, Roll AIDS, Walking AIDS, Medical AIDS, government AIDS, and most of all, monetary AIDS to their children!

OLD AGE IS GOLDEN

There is nothing the matter with me.
I'm healthy as can be.
I have arthritis in both of my knees.
And when I talk, I talk with a wheeze.
My pulse is weak and my blood is thin.
But I'm awfully well for the shape I'm in.

Arch supports I have for my feet.
Or I wouldn't be able to be on the street.
Sleep is denied me night after night.
But every morning I find I'm all right.
My memory is failing, my head's in a spin.
But I'm awfully fit for the shape I'm in.

How do I know that my youth is all spent?
Well, my 'get up and go', got up and went.
But I really don't mind when I think with a grin,
Of all the grand places my 'get up' has been.

Old age is golden, I've heard it said.
But sometimes I wonder as I get into bed,
With my ears in the drawer, my teeth in a cup,
My eyes on the table until I wake,
E're sleep comes o'er me, I say to myself,
'Is there anything else I should lay on the shelf?'

I'm awfully thankful for the shape I'm in.

A NEW WINE FOR SENIORS

California vintners in the Napa Valley area, which primarily produces Pino Blanc, Pinot Noir and Pinot Grigio wines, have developed a new hybrid grape that acts an an anti-diuretic. It is expected to reduce the number of trips older people have to make to the bathroom during the night.

The new wine will be marketed as Pino More.

~~~

Just in case you weren't feeling too old today, this will certainly change things.

The people who are starting college this fall across the antion were born in 1987. They are too young to remember the space shuttle blowing up. Their lifetime has always included AIDS. The CD was introduced the year they were born. They have always had an answering machine. They have always had cable. Jay Leno has always been on the Tonight Show. Popcorn has always been cooked in the microwave. They never took a swim and thought about Jaws. They don't know who Mork was or where he was from. They never heard, "Where's the Beef?", "I'd walk a mile for a Camel," or "de plane Boss, de plane." McDonald's never came in styrofoam containers. They don't have a clue how to use a typewriter.

Do you feel old yet?

OLDER THAN DIRT

"Hey Dad," one of my kids asked the other day, "What was your favourite fast food when you were growing up?"

Quips, Quotes, Zingers & One Liners
194

"We didn't have fast food when I was growing up," I informed him. "All the food was slow."

"C'mon, seriously, Dad...where did you eat?"

"It was a place called 'at home'," I explained. "Grandma cooked every day and when Grampa got home from work, we sat down together at the dining room table, and if I didn't like what she put on my plate I was allowed to sit there until I did like it."

By this time, the kid was laughing so hard I was afraid he was going to suffer serious internal damage, so I didn't tell him the part about how I had to have permission to leave the table. But here are some other things I would have told him about my childhood if I figured his system could have handled it:

Some parents never owned their own house, wore Levis, set foot on a golf course, traveled out of the country or had a credit card. In their later years, they had something called a revolving charge card. The card was good only at Sears Roebuck. Or maybe it was Sears and Roebuck. Either way, there is no Roebuck anymore. Maybe he died.

My parents never drove me to soccer practice. This was mosty because we never had heard of soccer. I had a bicycle that weighed probably 50 pounds, and only had one speed (slow). We didn't have a television in our house until I was 11, but my grandparents had one before that. It was, of course, black and white, but they bought a piece of coloured plastic to cover the screen. The top third was blue, like the sky, and the bottom third was green, like grass. The middle third was red. It was perfect for programs that had scenes of firetrucks riding across someone's lawn on a sunny day. Some people had a lens taped to the front of the TV to make the picutre look larger.

I was 13 before I tasted my first pizza. It was called 'pizza pie'. When I bit into it, I burned the roof of my mouth and the cheese slid off, swung down, plastered itself against my chin and burned that, too. It's still the best pizza I ever had.

We didn't have a car until I was 15. Before that, the only car in our family was my grandfather's Ford. He called it a 'machine'.

I never had a telephone in my room. The only phone in the house was in the living room and it was on a party line. Before you could dial, you had to listen to make sure some people you didn't know weren't already using the line.

Pizzas were not delivered to your home. But milk was.

All newspapers were delivered by boys and all boys delivered newspapers. I delivered a newspaper six days a week. It cost 7 cents a paper. I got to keep 2 cents. I had to get up at 4 a.m. every morning. On Saturday, I had to collect the 42 cents from my customers. My favourite customers were the ones who gave me 50 cents and told me to keep the change. My least favourite customers were the ones who seemed to never be home on collection day.

OLDER THAN DIRT QUIZ

Count all the ones that you remember, not the ones you were told about! Ratings are at the bottom.

1)   Blackjack chewing gum
2)   Wax Coke-shaped bottles with coloured sugar water
3)   Candy cigarettes
4)   Soda pop machines that dispensed glass bottles
5)   Coffee shops or diners with tableside juke boxes
6)   Home milk delivery in glass bottles with cardboard stoppers
7)   Party lines
8)   Newsreels before the movie
9)   P.F. Flyers
10)   Butch wax
11)   Telephone numbers with a word prefix (Olive-6933)
12)   Peashooters
13)   Howdy Doody
14)   45 RPM records
15)   S&H Green Stamps
16)   Hi-fi's
17)   Metal ice trays with lever
18)   Mimeograph paper
19)   Blue flashbulb
20)   Packards
21)   Roller skate keys
22)   Cork popguns

23) Drive-ins
24) Studebakers
25) Wash tub wringers

If you remembered 0 – 5, you're still young.
If you remembered 6 – 10, you're getting older.
If you remembered 11 – 15, don't tell your age!
If you remembered 16 – 25, you're older than dirt!

THE GOLDEN YEARS HAVE COME!

I cannot see, I cannot pee, I cannot chew, I cannot screw.
My memory shrinks. My hearing stinks.
No sense of smell. I look like hell.
My body's drooping. Got trouble pooping.

So, the golden years have come at last.
Well, the golden years can kiss my…

AGE DOESN'T MAKE YOU FORGETFUL. HAVING WAY TOO MANY STUPID THINGS TO REMEMBER MAKES YOU FORGETFUL.

Mid-Life is when you go to the doctor and you realize you are now so old you have to pay someone to look at you naked.

~~~

SENIOR DRESS CODE

Despite what you may have seen on the streets, the following combinations do not go together and should be avoided:

A nose ring and bifocals
Bikinis and liver spots
Spiked hair and bald spots
Short shorts and varicose veins
A pierced tonge and dentures
Midriff shirts and midriff bulge
Miniskirts and support hose
Unbuttoned disco shirts and a heart monitor
Ankle bracelets and corn pads
A belly button ring and a gall bladder surgery scar
Speedo's and cellulite
Inline skates and a walker
Things and Depends

SENIORS ON A LITTLE ROAD TRIP

While on a road trip, Joyce and Les stopped at a roadside restaurant for lunch. After finishing their meal, they left the restaurant and resumed their trip.

When leaving, Joyce unknowingly left her sunglasses on the table and she didn't miss them until they had been driving about twenty minutes.

By then, to add to the aggravation, they had to travel quite a distance before they could find a place to turn around in order to return to the restaurant to retrieve her glasses.

All the way back, Les became the classic grouchy old man. He fussed and complained and scolded Joyce relentlessly during the entire return drive. The more he chided her, the more agitated he became. He just wouldn't let up.

To Joyce's relieve, they finally arrived at the restaurant. As she got out of the car and hurried inside to retrieve her glasses, Les (the old geezer) yelled to her, "While you're in there, you might as well get my hat and credit card!"

20 THINGS LEARNED BY MIDDLEAGE

1) If you're too open-minded, your brains will fall out.

2) Don't worry about what people think; they don't do it very often.

3) Going to church doesn't make you a Christian any more than standing in a garage makes you a car.

4) It ain't the jeans that make your butt look fat.

5) Not one shred of evidence supports the notion that life is serious.

6) For every action, there is an equal and opposite government program.

7) If you look like your passport picture, you probably need the trip.

8) Bills travel through the mail at twice the speed of checks.

9) Eat well, stay fit, die anyway.

10) Men are from earth. Women are from earth. Deal with it.

11) No man has ever been shot while doing the dishes.

12) A balanced diet is a cookie in each hand.

13) Middleage is when broadness of the mind and narrowness of the waist change places.

14) Opportunities always look bigger going than coming.

15) Junk is something you've kept for years and throw away three weeks before you need it.

16) There is always one more imbecile than you counted on.

17) By the time you can make ends meet, they move the ends.

18) Thou shalt not weigh more than thy refrigerator.

19) Someone who thinks logically provides a nice contrast to the real world.

20) If you must choose between two evils, pick the one you've never tried before.

~~~

Quips, Quotes, Zingers & One Liners
199

Q: Grandma, were you on Noah's ark?
A: No.
Q: Then how did you survive the flood?

~~~

For the first time in many years, an old man traveled from his rural home to the city in order to see a movie. After buying his ticket, he stopped at the concession stand to purchase popcorn. Handing the attendant $3.50, he couldn't help but comment, "The last time I came to the movies, popcorn was only twenty-five cents."

"Well, sir," the attendant replied, "you're really going to enjoy yourself. The movies come with sound now."

~~~

"Look at me!" boasted a fit old man to a group of young people. "Each morning I do fifty push-ups, fifty sit-ups, and then walk two miles. I'm fit as a fiddle!"

"How do you do it?" one of the youngsters asked.

"Well, I don't smoke. I don't drink. I don't stay up late. And I don't chase after women. Thanks to all this clean living, tomorrow I'm going to celebrate my 95th birthday!"

"Oh really?" a skeptical onlooker asked, "How?"

~~~

Two men are sitting next to each other on a crowded downtown bus. The first man notices the second man has his eyes closed. "Hey, what's the matter?" he asks, "Are you sick?"

"No, I'm okay," the second man replies, "It's just that I hate to see old ladies standing."

~~~

When my grandfather was ill, my grandmother used to rub lard on his back. After that, he went downhill quickly.

~~~

Bernie was eating dinner at a friend's house. The friend prefaced every request to his wife with a sweet term of endearment: honey, darling, sweetheart, precious. When the wife left the room for a moment, Bernie turned to his friend and said, "You're such a sweet old fool. After all the years you've been married, it's a fine thing to keep calling your wife all those pet names."

"To tell you the truth," his friend replied, "I forgot her name seven years ago."

~~~

My nookie days are over,
My pistol light is out,
What used to be my sex appeal,
Is now my water spout.

Time was of its own accord,
From my trousers it would spring,
But now I've got a full-time job,
To find the blasted thing.

It used to be embarrasing,
The way it would behave,
For every single morning,
It would stand and watch me shave.

As my old age approaches,
It sure gives me the blues,
To see it hang its little head,
And watch me tie my shoes.

Inside every older person is a younger person wondering what the hell happened.

~~~

An old man was living out his days at a nursing home. One day the nurse noticed he was sad and depressed. She asked him, "Is there anything wrong?"

"Yes, nurse," the old man said, "my private part died today, and I am very sad."

Knowing her patients were sometimes a little senile, she replied, "Oh, I'm sorry, please accept my condolences."

The next day, the old man was walking down the hall with his penis hanging out of his pajamas. The nurse pulled him aside gently and said, "You shouldn't be walking down the hall like that. Please put your private part back inside your pajamas."

"But nurse," the old man protested, "I told you yesterday that my private part died."

"Yes, you did tell me that. But why is it hanging out of your pajamas?" the nurse asked.

"Well," he replied, "today is the viewing."

~~~

An old man was driving on the freeway and his mobile phone rang. His wife was on the line, her voice thick with anxiety. "Howard! I just saw on the news there's a car driving the wrong way on the freeway. Please be careful!"

"One?" replied Howard, "You've got to be kidding me. I see at least a hundred!"

~~~

An old man went to a brothel and asked the madam if he could spend the night with a young girl. Surprised, she asked how old he was, "I'm 90 years old," he replied proudly.

"Ninety!" the madam exclaimed. "Don't you realize you've had it?"

"Oh, sorry," the old man said, "How much do I owe you?"

~~~

You know you're over the hill when opportunity knocks but your hearing aid's turned off.

~~~

Heard in conversation over 40 years ago: "If they think I'll pay 30 cents for a haircut, forget it!"

~~~

Exercise: Droop Therapy

OXYMORONS

Is it good if a vacuum really sucks?

Why is the third hand on the watch called the second hand?

If a word is misspelled in the dictionary, how would we ever know?

If Webster wrote the first dictionary, where did he find the words?

Why do we say something is out of whack? What is a whack?

Why does "slow down" and "slow up" mean the same thing?

Why does "fat chance" and "slim chance" mean the same thing?

Why do "tug" boats push their barges?

Why do we sing "Take me out to the ballgame" when we are already there?

Why are they called "stands" when they are made for sitting?

Why is it called "after dark" when it is really "after light"?

Doesn't "expecting the unexpected" make the unexpected expected?

Why are "wise guy" and a "wise guy" opposite?

Why do "overlook" and "oversee" mean opposite things?

Why is "phonics" not spelled the way it sounds?

If work is so terrific, why do they have to pay you to do it?

If all the world is a stage, where is the audience sitting?

If love is blind, why is lingeries so popular?

If you are cross-eyed and have dyslexia, can you read all right?

Why do we put suits in garment bags and garments in a suitcase?

How come abbreviated is such a long word?

Why do we wash bath towels? Aren't we clean when we use them?

Why doesn't glue stick to the inside of the bottle?

Why do they call it a TV set when you only have one?

Christmas – what other time of year do you sit in front of a dead tree and eat candy out of your socks?

PANIC

A woman was flying from Seattle to San Francisso on Southwest Airlines. Unexpectedly, the plane was diverted to Sacramento along the way. The flight attendant explained that there would be a delay, and if the passengers wanted to get off the aircraft the plane would reboard in 50 minutes.

Everybody got off the plane except one lady who was blind. The man had noticed her as he walked by and could tell the lady was blind because her Seeing Eye dog lay quietly underneath the seats in front of her throughout the entire flight.

He could also tell she had flown this very flight before because the pilot approached her, and calling her by name, said, "Kathy, we are in Sacramento for almost an hour. Would you like to get off and stretch your legs?"

The blind lady replied, "No thanks, but maybe Buddy would like to stretch his legs."

All the people in the gate area came to a complete standstill when they looked up and saw the pilot walk off the plane with a Seeing Eye dog!

The pilot was even wearing sunglasses. People scattered. They not only tried to change planes, but they were trying to change airlines!

True story!

PHILOSOPHICAL

When we ask for advice, we are usually looking for an accomplice.

Tact is giving a person a shot in the arm without letting him feel the needle.

The genius resides in the capacity for evaluation of uncertain, hazardous and conflicting information.

Fear cannot be banished, but it can be calm and without panic; it can be mitigated by reason and evaluation.

A blunder at the right moment is better than cleverness at the wrong time.

I am more fond of achieving, than striving. My theories must prove to be facts or be discarded as worthless. My efforts must soon be crowned with success or be discontinued.

If you don't know where you're going, any road will take you there.

~~~

Last week, I stated this woman was the ugliest woman I had ever seen. I have since been visited by her sister, and now wish to withdraw that statement.
Mark Twain

The secret of a good sermon is to have a good beginning and a good ending; and to have the two as close together as possible.
George Burns

By the time a man is wise enough to watch his step, he's too old to go anywhere.
Billy Crystal

By all means, marry. If you get a good wife, you'll become happy. If you get a bad one, you'll become a philosopher.
Socrates

I never drink water because of the disgusting things that fish do in it.
W.C. Fields

I don't feel old. I don't feel anything until noon. Then it's time for my nap.
Bob Hope

My luck is so bad that if I bought a cemetary, people would stop dying.
Rodney Dangerfield

Only Irish coffee provides in a single glass all four essential food groups – alcohol, caffeine, sugar and fat.
Alex Levine

Money can't buy you happiness...but it does bring you a more pleasant form of misery.
Spike Milligan

I was married by a judge. I should have asked for a jury.
Groucho Marx

Until I was thirteen, I thought my name was Shut Up.
Joe Namath

My wife has a slight impediment in her speech. Every now and then she stops to breathe.
Jimmy Durante

Maybe it's true that life begins at fifty...but everything else starts to wear out, fall out, or spread out...
Phyllis Diller

I have never hated a man enough to give his diamonds back.
Zsa Zsa Gabor

Santa Claus has the right idea. Visit people only once a year.
Victor Borge

Sometimes when I look at my children, I say to myself, "Lillian, you should have remained a virgin..."
Lillian Carter (mother of Jimmy Carter)

We could certainly slow the aging process down if it had to work its way through Congress
Will Rogers

Don't worry about avoiding temptation. As you grow older, it will avoid you.
Winston Churchill

Everybody's got to believe in something. I believe I'll have another beer.
W.C. Fields

Too bad all the people who know how to run this country are busy driving taxicabs or cutting hair.
George Burns

We know what a person thinks, not when he tells us what he thinks, but by his actions.
Isaac Bashevis Singer

If you tell the truth, you don't have to remember anything.
Mark Twain

Don't go around saying the world owes you a living. The world owes you nothing. It was here first.
Mark Twain

Age does not protect you from love. But love, to some extent, protects you from age.
Jeanne Moreau

There are 350 varieties of shark, not counting loan and pool.
L.M. Boyd

Those are my principals. If you don't like them, I have others.
Groucho Marx

When a man steals your wife, there is no better revenge than to let him keep her.
David Bissonette

Two secrets to keep your marriage brimming:
1) Whenever you're wrong, admit it.
2) Whenever you're right, shut up.
Patrick Murra

There's a way of transferring funds that is even faster than electronic banking. It's called marriage.
Sam Kinison

Quips, Quotes, Zingers & One Liners

The great question, which I have not been able to answer....is, "What does a woman want?"
Dumas

~~~

And the cardiologist's diet – if it tastes good, spit it out.

May your troubles be less, may your blessings be more, and may nothing but happiness come through your door.

Knowledge is knowing a tomato is a fruit. Wisdom is not using it in a fruit salad.

I no longer skinny dip. I chunky dunk.

I never met a calorie I didn't like.

Middleage is when a broad mind and a narrow waist change places.

I'm not overweight, I'm undertall.

He who laughs last, thinks slowest.

Don't put off until tomorrow what you can do today. You may like it and want to do it again.

Aspire to inspire before you expire.

To err is human, to blame it on someone else shows management potential.

Success is the best revenge.

Earth is the insane asylum for the universe.

I'm not bossy, I just have better ideas.

Wine a little, it'll make you feel better.

I can only please one person per day. Today is not your day and tomorrow doesn't look any better.

Happiness is a choice.

If it is true that we're here to help others, what are the others here for?

Team effort – a lot of people doing what I say.

~~~

A turkey was chatting with a bull. "I would love to be able to get to the top of that tree," sighed the turkey, "but I haven't got the energy."

"Well, why don't you nibble on some of my droppings?" replied the bull. "They're packed with nutrients."

The turkey pecked at the lump of dung, and found it actually gave him enough strength to reach the lowest branch of the tree.

The next day, after eating some more dung, he reached the second branch.

Finally, after a fourth night, the turkey was proudly perched at the top of the tree. He was promptly spotted by a farmer, who shot him out of the tree.

Moral of the story: bullshit might get you to the top, but it won't keep you there.

~~~

In just two days from now, tomorrow will be yesterday.

A bartender is just a pharmacist with a limited inventory.

My short-term memory is not as sharp as it used to be. Also, my short-term memory's not as sharp as it used to be.

I may be schizophrenic, but at least I have each other.

If you don't spread your wings, you'll never know how far you can fly.

I don't know what tomorrow holds. I just know who holds it.

Don't cry because it's over, smile because it happened.

A truly happy person is one who can enjoy the scenery on a detour.

Happiness comes through doors you didn't even know you left open.

I refuse to have a battle of wits with an unarmed person.

In the olden days, you could see two movies for a dime. Now you pay $500 for a TV to watch those same movies.

Most people would be satisfied with enough, as long as other people didn't have more.

Birthdays are good for you, the more you have, the longer you live.

Considering how good a shot Cupid is with the bow and arrow, it's amazing how many bad Mrs. he's had.

How long a minute is depends on what side of the bathroom door you're on.

If ignorance is bliss, why aren't more people happy?

If you can't say something nice about someone, please report to personnel immediately.

An oldtimer is someone who remembers when 'Five and Ten' stood for cents, and not dollars.

Can a contortionist foresee their own end?

Have you ever had the feeling that your career is on hold, when really it's been discontinued?

The only trouble with a second childhood is that you can't blame anything on your parents.

You may be only one person in the world, but you may also be the world to one person.

Some mistakes are too much fun to only make once.

We could learn a lot from crayons: some are sharp, some are pretty, some are dull, some have weird names, and all are different colors...but they all have to learn to live in the same box.

No one ever says "It's only a game" when their team is winning.

A good time to keep your mouth shut is when you're in deep water.

Be careful about reading the fine print...there's no way you're going to like it.

Lord, keep your arms around my shoulder and your hand over my mouth.

Woman inspires us to great things, and prevents us from achieving them.

Laugh and the world laughs with you, snore and you sleep alone.

Success is relative. The more the success, the more relatives.

When I read about the evils of drinking....I gave up reading.

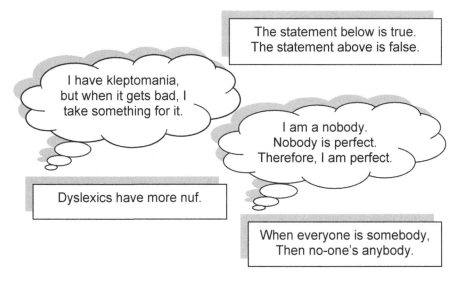

The statement below is true.
The statement above is false.

I have kleptomania, but when it gets bad, I take something for it.

I am a nobody.
Nobody is perfect.
Therefore, I am perfect.

Dyslexics have more nuf.

When everyone is somebody,
Then no-one's anybody.

I define spin as mankind's attempt to put its best foot forward. Lovers are master spinners. So are job applicants. Doctors spin all the time, often to comfort the patient or family. Lawyers spin when they present their case.

I'm convinced that the human brain is hardwired to spin, to persuade others to your point of view. Bad spin is mean-spirited, opportunistic, sleazy. Good spin is being smart but also being on the level. Good spin sticks with reality.

~~~

It's always darkest before the dawn. So, if you're going to steal your neighbour's newspaper, that's the time to do it.

Don't be irreplaceable; if you can't be replaced, you can't be promoted.

Always remember you're unique, just like everyone else.

Never test the depth of the water with both feet.

If may be that your sole purpose in life is simply to serve as a warning to others.

If you think nobody cares if you're alive, try missing a couple of car payments.

Before you criticize someone, you should walk a mile in their shoes. That way, when you criticize them, you're a mile away and you have their shoes.

~~~

It's not easy...
To apologize.
To begin over.
To take advice.
To be unselfish.
To admit an error.
To face a sneer.

To be charitable.
To keep trying.
To be considerate.
To avoid mistakes.
To endure success.
To profit by mistakes.
To forgive and forget.
To think and then act.
To keep out of a rut.
To make the best of little
To subdue an unruly temper.
To shoulder a deserved blame.
To recognize the silver lining.
But it always pays!!

If passion drives you, let reason be the steering wheel.

~~~

Is it true that you never really learn to swear until you learn to drive?

~~~

RULES FOR BEING HUMAN

1)   You will receive a body. You may like it or hate it, but it will be yours for the entire period this time around.

2)   You will learn lessons. You are enrolled in a full-time informal school called life. Each day in this school you will have the opportunity to learn lessons. You may like the lessons or think them irrelevant and stupid.

3)   There are no mistakes, only lessons. Growth is a process of trial and error, experimentation. The 'failed' experiments are as much a part of the process as the experiment that ultimately 'works'.

4)   A lesson is repeated until learned. A lesson will be presented to you in various forms until you have learned it. When you have learned it, you can then go on to the next lesson.

5)   Learning lessons does not end. There is no part of life that does not contain its lessons. If you are alive, there are lessons to be learned.

6) 'There' is no better than 'here'. When your 'there' has become a 'here' you will simply obtain another 'there' that will, again, look better than 'here'.

7) Others are merely mirrors of you. You cannot love or hate something about another person unless it reflects to you something you love or hate about yourself.

8) What you make of your life is up to you. You have all the tools and resources you need. What you do with them is up to you. The chance is yours.

9) Your answers lie inside you. The answers to life's questions lie inside you. All you need to do is look, listen, and trust.

~~~

Tomorrow – one of the greatest labour saving devices of today.

We can't become what we need to be by remaining what we are.

When all else fails, pay attention!

Indecision and delays are the parents of failure.

I used to be indecisive. Not I'm not sure.

Neither success nor failure is permanent.

If you don't stand for something, you'll fall for anything.

I'm not saying you're stupid. I'm just saying you've got bad luck when it comes to thinking.

Is there ever a day that mattresses are not on sale?

Work, luck and hard are all four letter words.

It's not the years in your life that count, it's the life in your years.

If you don't make mistakes, you don't make anything.

Success is the ability to go from failure to failure without a loss of enthusiasm.

Making mistakes is better than doing nothing.

Being right half the time is better than being half-right all the time.

Don't count the days. Make the days count.

Marriage is like a deck of cards. In the beginning all you need is two hearts and a diamond. By the end, you wish you had a club and a spade.

When I woke up this morning...no wrinkles in sight, the house was spotless, the garden looked lovely, and my grumpy bloke looked like George Clooney. I don't think I'll ever put my glasses on again.

Some people just need a hug....around the neck....with a rope.

Life is too short to stress yourself with people who don't even deserve to be an issue in your life.

Things turn out the best for people who make the best of the way things turn out.

You can't always control who walks into your life...but you can control which window you throw them out of.

Some people come into our lives and leave footprints on our hearts. Others come along and we want to leave footprints on their face.

Starting tomorrow, whatever life throws at me, I'm gonna duck so it hits someone else.

Forget what hurt you in the past. But never forget what it taught you.

Teachers open the door. You enter by yourself.

Don't bother about people who judge you without knowing you...remember, dogs bark if they don't know the person.

~~~

Your true soul mate can see the sorrow behind your smile,
The love behind your anger,
And the reason behind your silence.

Forgiveness does not change the past but it does enlarge the future.

POINT OF VIEW

BILL GATES AND GM

From Bill Gates, "If GM had kept up with technology, like the computer industry has, we would all be driving $25 cars that got 1000 miles to the gallon."

In response to Bill Gates' comments, GM issued a press release stating if GM had developed technology like Microsoft, we would all be driving cars with the following characteristics:

- For no reason whatsoever your car would crash twice a day.

- Every time they repainted the line on the road you would have to buy a new car.

- Occasionally your car would die on the freeway for no reason and you would just accept this, restart and drive on.

- Occasionally, executing a manoeuvre such as a left turn, would cause your car to shut down and refuse to start in which case you would have to reinstall the engine.

- Only one person at a time could use the car unless you bought "car 95" or "car NT". But then you would have to buy more seats.

- MacIntosh would make a car that was powered by the sun, reliable, 5 times as fast and twice as easy to drive but would only run on 5% of the roads.

- The oil, temperature and alternator warning light would be replaced by a single "general default" warning light.

- The air bag system would say "are you sure?" before going off.

- Occasionally, and for no reason whatsoever, your car would lock you out and refuse to let you in until you simultaneously lifted the door handle, turned the key and grabbed hold of the radio antenna.

- GM would require all car buyers to also purchase a complete set of Rand McNally road maps (a GM subsidiary) even though they neither need them or want them. Attempting to delete this system would immediately cause the car's performance to decrease by 50% or more. Moreover, GM would become a target for the Justice Department.

Quips, Quotes, Zingers & One Liners

- Every time GM introduced a new model, drivers would have to learn to drive all over again because none of the controls would operate in the same manner as the old car. You'd press the start button to shut off the engine.

> The best Super Bowl is not the NFL showpiece.
> It's a toilet bowl which cleans itself.

COPS

These police comments were taken off actual police car videos around the country. Thank goodness, in spite of the perils of the job, they still have a sense of humor!

"You know, stop lights don't come any redder than the one you just went through."

"Relax, the handcuffs are tight because they're new. They'll stretch after you wear them for a while."

"If you take your hands off the car, I'll make your birth certificate a worthless document."

"If you run, you'll only go to jail tired."

"Can you run faster than 1200 feet per second? Because that's the speed of the bullet that'll be chasing you."

"You don't know how fast you were going? I guess that means I can write anything I want to on the ticket, huh?"

"Yes, sir, you can talk to the shift supervisor, but I don't think it will help you. Oh, did I mention that I'm the shift supervisor."

"Warning! You want a warning? Okay, I'm warning you not to do that again or I'll give you another ticket."

"The answer to this last question will determine whether you are drunk or not. Was Mickey Mouse a cat or a dog?"

"Fair? You want me to be fair? Listen, fair is a place where you go to ride on rides, eat cotton candy and corn dogs and step in monkey shit."

"Yeah, we have a quota. Two more tickets and my wife gets a toaster oven."

"In God we trust, all others we run through NCIC."

"How big were those 'two beers' you say you had?"

"No sir, we don't have quotas anymore. We used to, but now we're allowed to write as many tickets as we can."

"I'm glad to hear that the Chief of Police is a personal friend of yours. So you know someone who can post your bail..."

POLITICIANS

One day a florist went to a barber for a haircut.

After the cut, he asked about his bill, and the barber replied, "I cannot accept money from you, I'm doing community service this week." The florist was pleased and left the shop.

When the barber went to open his shop the next morning, there was a 'thank you' card and a dozen roses waiting for him at his door.

Later, a cop comes in for a haircut, and when he tries to pay his bill, the barber again replied, "I cannot accept the money from you, I'm doing community service this week." The cop was happy and lef the shop.

The next morning when the barber went to open up, there was a 'thank you' card and a dozen donuts waiting for him at his door.

Then a Member of Parliament came in for a haircut, and when he went to pay his bill, the barber again replied, "I can not accept money from you. I'm doing community service this week." The MP was very happy and left the shop.

The next morning, when the barber went to open up, there was a dozen MP's lined up waiting for a free haircut.

And that, my friends, illustrates the fundamental difference between the citizens of our country and the politicians who run it.

~~~

Next year will mark the beginning of a new reality n Ottawa and Washington. There will be no Nativity scene at Christmas. Three wise men cannot be found. The search for a virgin has been abandoned. However, there are plenty of asses for the stable.

A man died and went to Heaven. As he stood in front of the Pearly Gates, he saw a huge wall of clocks behind him.

He asked, "What are all those clocks?"

St. Peter answered, "Those are lie-clocks. Everyone who has ever been on earth has a lie-clock. Every time you lie, the hands on your clock move."

"Oh," said the man. "Whose clock is that?"

"That's Mother Teresa's," replied St. Peter. "The hands have never moved, indicating that she never told a lie."

"Incredible," said the man, "And whose clock is that one?"

St. Peter responded, "That's Abraham Lincoln's clock. The hands have moved twice, telling us that Abraham told only two lies in his entire life."

"My local politician died recently. Where's his clock?"

St. Peter replied, "Jesus has it in his office. He uses it as a ceiling fan."

PONDERISMS

Why do you need a driver's license to buy liquor when you can't drink and drive?

Why are there interstate highways in Hawaii?

Why are there floatation devices under plane seats instead of parachutes?

Why are cigarettes sold in gas stations when smoking is prohibited there?

Do you need a silencer if you are going to shoot a mime?

Have you ever imagined a world with no hypothetical situations?

How does the guy who drives the snowplow get to work in the mornings?

If 7-11 is open 24 hours a day, 365 days a year, why are there locks on the doors?

If a cow laughed, would milk come out her nose?

If nothing ever sticks to Teflon, how do they make Teflon stick to the pan?

If you tied buttered toast to the back of a cat and dropped it from a height, what would happen?

If you're in a vehicle going the speed of light, what happens when you turn on the headlights?

If heterosexuals are straight, are homosexuals bent?

Why is it that no plastic bag will open from the end on your first try?

Whatever happened to Preparations A through G?

Why do Kamikaze pilots wear helmets?

Why do they put up pictures of criminals in the Post Office? Are you supposed to write them? Why don't they just put their pictures on the postage stamps so the mailmen can look for them while they deliver the mail?

What do you get when you cross a snowman with a vampire? Frostbite.

Why doesn't the glue stick to the inside of the bottle?

Do you ever wonder why you gave me your email address?

Health is merely the slowest possible rate at which one can die.

Why is there a light in the fridge and not in the freezer?

If quizzes are quizzical, what are test?

Do illiterate people get the full effect of Alphabet Soup?

How is it one careless match can start a bushfire, but it takes a whole box to start a campfire?

Who was the first person to look at a cow and say, "I think I'll squeeze these dangly things here, and drink whatever comes out?"

Who was the first person to say, "See that chicken there? I'm going to eat the next thing that comes out of its arse."

In the 60's, people took acid to make the world weird. Now the world is weird and people take Prozac to make it normal.

The only difference between a groove and a grave is the depth.

Health nuts are going to feel stupid someday, lying in hospitals dying of nothing.

Have you noticed since everyone has a camcorder these days no one talks about seeing UFO's like they used to.

Whenever I feel blue, I start breathing again.

All of us could take a lesson from the weather. It pays no attention to criticism.

A day without sunshine is like night.

On the other hand, you have different fingers.

PSYCHIATRISTS

Why do psychiatrists give their patients shock treatment?
To prepare them for the bill.

Psychiatrist: You're crazy.
Patient: I'd like a second opinion.
Psychiatrist: All right. You're also ugly.

A man went to see a psychiatrist and said, "I just can't seem to make friends. Can you help me, you fat slob?"

Two psychiatrists passed in the corridor. The first said, "Hello." The second thought, 'I wonder what he meant by that..."

A psychiatrist congratulated his patient on making excellent progress. "You call this progress?" snapped the patient. "Six months ago, I was Napoleon. Now I'm nobody!"

A patient told his psychiatrist, "I always have this weird dream at night. I am locked in a room, and there is this door with a sign on it. I try to push the door with all my strength, but no matter how hard I try it simply won't budge."
"Interesting," mused the psychiatrist, "Tell me, what does the sign on the door say?"
The patient replied, "It says 'Pull'."

A man phoned the psychiatrist at the local mental hospital and asked, "Who's in Room 18."
"Nobody," said the psychiatrist.
"Good," said the man. "I must have escaped."

A woman walked into a psychiatrist's office and said, "I need help. I think I could be a nymphomaniac?"
"Well, I might be able to help you," said the psychiatrist, "but I must warn you that I charge $100 an hour."
"That's fair," said the woman. "How much do you charge for the night?"

Did you hear about the man who suffered from paranoia and low self-esteem?
He thought no one important was out to get him.

A man had become convinced that he was a dog, so he went to see a psychiatrist.

"It's terrible," said the man, "I walk around on all fours, I keep barking in the middle of the night and I can't walk past a lamp post any more."
"Very well," said the psychiatrist, "Get on the couch."
The man said, "I'm not allowed on the couch!"

A man walked into a psychiatrist's office with a pancake on his head, a burger on each shoulder, a strip of bacon over each ear and a strand of spaghetti up his nose.
"How can I help you?" asked the psychiatrist.
The man said, "I'm worried about my brother."

A doctor was doing his rounds at a psychiatric hospital when he arrived at a room occupied by two patients. One patient was sawing an imaginary plank of wood while the other was hanging from the ceiling.
"What's he doing up there?" asked the doctor.
"He thinks he's a light bulb," replied the patient who was doing the sawing.
"Shouldn't you get him down?" said the doctor. "He might hurt himself."
"What? And work in the dark?"

A man walked into a psychiatrist's office and said, "My wife thinks I'm crazy because I like sausages."
"That's nonsense," said the psychiatrist. "I like sausages, too."
"Great," said the man, "You must come and see my collection – I've got hundreds of them."

Two psychologists meet at their 25th college reunion. One of them looks young and energetic, while the other looks old and aged. The older-looking one asks the other, "What's your secret? Listening to other people's problems every day for so many years has made an old man of me."
The other replies, "Who listens?"

Q: How many psychiatrists does it take to change a lightbulb?
A: None. The lightbulb will change itself, when it's ready.

Q: How many psychiatrists does it take to change a lightbulb?
A: How long have you been having this fantasy?

Q: How many psychiatrists does it take to change a lightbulb?
A: How many do you think it takes?

Two psychologists have sex. One turns to the other and says, "That was good for you. How was it for me?"

PUNS

An invisible man marries an invisible woman. The kids were nothing to look at either.

~~~

A set of jump leads walk into a bar. The bartender says, "I'll serve you, but don't start anything."

~~~

Shelley, a talent scout for a large recording studio, was walking by a convent when he heard someone singing in a voice so beautiful he couldn't believe his ears. He rang the bell and asked to speak to the woman with the amazing voice. Soon a young nun appeared. "Sister," Shelley said, "I represent Euphonics, Inc., and I'd like you to make a tape of hymns. Your fee could be donated to charity."
"I'd be delighted," she replied, "but first I must get written permission from our Mother Superior."
"Okay, Sister, just give me a call."
Shelley rushed back to the office and described his find to his boss. Then he asked for a raise. Replied the boss, "Wait 'till the nun signs, Shelley."

PUNS FOR THE STUDIOUS AND LYRICAL

1) King Ozymandias of Assyria was running low on cash after years of war with the Hittites. His last great possession was the Star of the Euphrates, the most valuable diamond in the ancient world. Desperate, he went to Croesus, the pawnbroker, to ask for a loan.

   Croesus said, "I'll give you 100,000 dinars for it."

   "But I paid a million dinars for it," the King protested. "Don't you know who I am? I am the king!"

   Croesus replied, "When you wish to pawn a Star, makes no difference who you are."

2) Evidence has been found that William Tell and his family were avid bowlers. Unfortunately, all the Swiss league records were destroyed in a fire ...and so we'll never know for whom the Tells bowled.

3) A man rushed into a busy doctor's office and shouted, "Doctor! I think I'm shrinking!" The doctor calmly responded, "Now, settle down. You'll just have to be a little patient."

4) A marine biologist developed a race of genetically engineered dolphins that could live forever if they were fed a steady diet of seagulls. One day, his supply of the birds ran out so he had to go out and trap some more. On the way back, he spied two lions asleep on the road. Afraid to wake them, he gingerly stepped over them. Immediately, he was arrested and charged with-- transporting gulls across sedate lions for immortal porpoises.

5) Back in the 1800's the Tate's Watch Company of Massachusetts wanted to produce other products, and since they already made the cases for watches, they decided to produce compasses. The new compasses were so bad that people often ended up in Canada or Mexico rather than California. This, of course, is the origin of the expression -- "He who has a Tate's is lost!"

6) A thief broke into the local police station and stole all the toilets and urinals, leaving no clues. A spokesperson was quoted as saying, "We have absolutely nothing to go on."

7) An Indian chief was feeling very sick, so he summoned the medicine man. After a brief examination, the medicine man took out a long, thin strip of elk rawhide and gave it to the chief, telling him to bite off, chew, and swallow one inch of the leather every day. After a month, the medicine man returned to see how the chief was feeling. The chief shrugged and said, "The thong is ended, but the malady lingers on."

8) A famous Viking explorer returned home from a voyage and found his name missing from the town register. His wife insisted on complaining to the local civic official who apologized profusely saying, "I must have taken Leif off my census."

9) There were three Indian squaws. One slept on a deer skin, one slept on an elk skin, and the third slept on a hippopotamus skin. All three became pregnant. The first two each had a baby boy. The one who slept on the hippopotamus skin had twin boys. This just goes to prove that.. the squaw of the hippopotamus is equal to the sons of the squaws of the other two hides.

10) A skeptical anthropologist was cataloguing South American folk remedies with the assistance of a tribal Brujo who indicated that the leaves of a particular fern were a sure cure for any case of constipation. When the anthropologist expressed his doubts, the Brujo looked him in the eye and said, "Let me tell you, with fronds like these, you don't need enemas."

~~~

What was the name of the Russian who invented a cure for the common cold?
Benylin Forchestikov

~~~

Following the theft of a truck full of toupees, police officers were reported to be combing the area.

~~~

David Hasselhoff walked into a bar and ordered a beer. The bartender said, "It's a pleasure to serve you, Mr. Hasselhoff."

"Just call me Hoff," said the actor.

"Sure," said the bartender. "No hassle."

~~~

How do you catch a unique rabbit?
Unique up on it!

How do you catch a tame rabbit?
Tame way. Unique up on it.

~~~

How do crazy people go through the forest?
They take the psycho-path.

~~~

A woman has twins, and gives them up for adoption.

One of them goes to a family in Egypt, and is named 'Ahmal'.

The other goes to a family in Spain and they name him 'Juan'.

Years later, Juan sends a picture of himself to his birth mother. Upon receiving the picture, she tells her husband that she wishes she also had a picture of Ahmal.

Her husband responds, "They're twins! If you've seen Juan, you've seen Ahmal."

~~~

Two Eskimos sitting in a kayak were a bit cold, so they lit a fire in the craft. It sank, proving once again that you can't have your kayak and heat it too.

~~~

A group of chess enthusiasts checked into a hotel, and were standing in the lobby discussing their recent tournament victories. After about an hour, the manager came out of the office and asked them to disperse.

"But why," they asked as they moved off.

"Because," he said, "I can't stand chess-nuts boasting in an open foyer."

~~~

What do you call a fish with no eyes?
A fsh.

~~~

- Jokes about German sausage are wurst.
- Velcro – what a rip off!
- I tried to catch some fog. I mist.
- The Energizer bunny was arrested and charged with battery.
- The old man didn't like his beard at first. Then it grew on him.

- They told me I had type A blood, but it was a type-O.
- I did a theatrical performance about puns. It was a play on words.
- Did you hear about the cross-eyed teacher who lost her job because she couldn't control her pupils?
- What do you call a dinosaur with an extensive vocabulary? A thesaurus.
- What does a clock do when it's hungry. It goes back for seconds.
- When you get a bladder infection, urine trouble.
- This girl said she recognized me from the vegetarian club, but I'd never met herbivore.
- I used to be a banker, but then I lost interest.
- Venison for dinner? Oh deer!
- Why were the Indians here first? They had reservations.
- Broken pencils are pointless.
- England has no kidney bank, but it does have a Liverpool.
- How does Moses make his tea? Hebrews it.
- Earthquake in Washington obviously government's fault.
- Cartoonist found dead in home. Details are sketchy.
- I got a job at a bakery because I kneaded dough.
- I stayed up all night to see where the sun went. Then it dawned on me.
- When chemists die, they barium.
- I changed my iPod's name to Titanic. It's syncing now.
- I know a guy who's addicted to brake fluid. He says he can stop anytime.
- We're going on a class trip to the Coca-Cola factory. I hope there's no pop quiz.
- I dropped out of communism class because of lousy Marx.
- Haunted French pancakes give me the crepes.
- Be kind to your dentist. He has fillings, too.

~~~

Mahatma Ghandi, as you know, walked barefoot most of the time, which produced an impressive set of calluses on his feet.

He also ate very little, which made him rather frail and with his odd diet, he suffered from bad breath.

This made him (oh man, this is so bad…it's good) a super-calloused fragile mystic hexed by halitosis.

PUTDOWNS

Our complaint manager is Helen Waite.
If you have a complaint, go to Helen Waite.

~~~

A man in a hot air balloon realized he was lost. He reduced altitude and spotted a woman below.

He descended a bit more and shouted, "Excuse me, can you help me? I promised a friend I would meet him an hour ago and I don't know where I am?"

The woman replied, "You're in a hot air balloon hovering approximately 30 feet above ground. You're between 40 and 41 degrees north latitude and between 59 and 60 degrees west longitude."

"You must be a mathematician," said the balloonist.

"I am," replied the woman, "How did you know?"

"Well," answered the balloonist, "everything you told me is probably technically correct, but I have no idea what to make of your information and the fact is, I'm still lost. Frankly, you've not been much help at all. If anything, you've delayed my trip."

The woman responded, "You must be in management."

"I am," replied the balloonist, "but how did you know?"

"Well," said the woman, "you don't know where you are or where you're going. You have risen to where you are due to a large quantity of hot air. You made a promise, which you've no idea how to keep, and you expect people beneath you to solve your problems. The fact is you are in exactly the same position you were in before we met, but now, somehow, it is my fault."

Some people can have all the lights on and still be in the dark.

I believe that everything happens for a reason. Usually, the reason is that somebody screwed up.

I'd consider hormone replacement therapy, but I've got a bunch of other things that need to be replaced first.

What's your secret for keeping your figure?
Getting everything to droop at the same rate.

You ARE REGRETFULLY INVITED
TO THE WEDDING BETWEEN MY PERFECT SON,

The Doctor

AND SOME

Cheap Two-Bit Tramp

WHOSE NAME ESCAPES ME RIGHT NOW.

THE BIGGEST DISASTER IN MY
FAMILY'S HISTORY WILL TAKE PLACE AT

9pm on Saturday, September 8th

AND NO DOUBT END IN DIVORCE.
HOPEFULLY IN TIME TO STILL BE ELIGIBLE FOR AN ANNULMENT.
THE OVERWHELMINGLY DISAPPOINTING HEARTBREAK OF A CEREMONY
WILL BE FOLLOWED BY DINNER, WHERE NUTS WILL BE SERVED
BECAUSE WHATSHERFACE HAS AN ALLERGY.

SNOTTY RECEPTIONIST

An older gentleman had an appointment to see the urologist who shared offices with several other doctors. The waiting room was filled with patients.

As he approached the receptionist desk he noticed that the receptionist was a large, unfriendly woman who looked like a Sumo wrestler. He gave her his name.

In a very loud voice, the receptionist said, "Yes, I have your name here. You want to see the doctor about impotence, right?"

All the patients in the waiting room snapped their heads around to look at the very embarrrassed man. He recovered quicky, and in an equally loud voice replied, "No, I've come to inquire about a sex change operation, but I don't want the same doctor that did yours."

Why Computers Are Female

- No one but their creator understands their internal logic.
- They hear what you say, but not what you mean.
- Even your smallest mistakes are immediately committed to memory for future reference.
- You do the same thing for years, and suddenly it's wrong.

Why Computers Are Male

- In order to get their attention, you have to turn them on.
- They have a lot of data but still are clueless.
- They are supposed to help you solve problems, but half the time they are the problem.
- As soon as you commit to one you realize that if you had waited a little longer you could have had a better model.

~~~

How can a woman stop her husband from reading her emails?
Rename the file "Instruction Manuals".

~~~

What's the best way to tune a banjo?
With wire cutters.

~~~

A woman was looking through the frozen turkeys at a supermarket but couldn't find one big enough to feed her family.

She asked a stock boy, "Do these turkeys get any bigger?"

"No, ma'am," he replied. "They're dead."

QUOTES

If you had your life to live over again, don't do it.

An elderly man approaches a prostitute, "How about a little fun?"
She says, "How old are you?"
He says, "Eighty."
She says, "You've already had it."
He says, "How much do I owe you?"

A man seventy-five years old is reading in his hotel room when he hears a knock on the door and a beautiful girl says, "I'm sorry, I must be in the wrong room."
He says, "You got the right room, but you're forty years too late."

Some people bring happiness wherever they go. You bring happiness *whenever* you go.

One time I came home and my wife was crying because the dog had eaten a pie she made for me.
"Don't cry," I told her, "I'll buy you another dog."

An elderly man was visiting his doctor for a check-up. The doctor said, "Mr. Jones, you're sound as a dollar. You'll live to be eighty."
"But I am eighty," Mr. Jones says.
"See, what did I tell you?"

A woman called up the Police Department and said, "I have a sex maniac in my apartment. Pick him up in the morning."

A man goes to the shrink and tells him that no one talks to him.
The doctor says, "Next."

A doctor asked his woman patient, "Do you know what the most effective birth control pill is?"
She replied, "No."
He said, "That's it!"

A man fell out of a tenth-story window. He's lying on the ground with a big crowd around him, a cop walks over and says, "What happened?"
The guy says, "I don't know, I just got here."

Two newlyweds – he's 64 and she's 23. She catches him cheating with a 48-year old woman.
She says, "What has she got I haven't got?"
He says, "Patience!"

Quips, Quotes, Zingers & One Liners
259

George W. Bush Quotes

The vast majority of our imports come from outside the country.

If we don't succeed, we run the risk of failure.

Republicans understand the importance of bondage between a mother and child.

No senior citizen should ever have to choose between prescription drugs and medicine.

I believe we are on an irreversible trend toward more freedom and democracy – but that could change.

One word sums up probably the responsibility of any Governor, and that one word is 'to be prepared.'

Verbosity leads to unclear, inarticulate things.

I have made good judgments in the past. I have made good judgments in the future.

The future will be better tomorrow.

We're going to have the best educated American people in the world.

One of the great things about books is sometimes there are some fantastic pictures. (during an education photo-op)

Illegitimacy is something we should talk about in terms of not having it.

We are ready for any unforeseen event that may or may not occur.

It isn't pollution that's harming the environment. It's the impurities in our air and water that are doing it.

Great Quotes by Great Ladies

Inside every older person is a younger person – wondering what the hell happened.
Cora Harvey Armstrong

The hardest years in life are those between ten and seventy.
Helen Hayes (at 73)

I refuse to think of them as chin hairs. I think of them as stray eyebrows.
Janette Barber

Things are going to be a lot worse before they get worse.
Lily Tomlin

A male gynecologist is like an auto mechanic who never owned a car.
Carrie Snow

Laugh and the world laughs with you. Cry and you cry with your girlfriends.
Laurie Kuslansky

My second favorite household chore is ironing. My first being hitting my head on the top bunk until I faint.
Erma Bombeck

Old age ain't no place for sissies.
Bette Davis

A man's got to do what a man's got to do. A woman must do what he can't.
Rhonda Hansome

The phrase "working mother" is redundant.
Jane Sellman

Every time I close the door on reality, it comes in through the windows.
Jennifer Unlimited

Whatever women must do they must do it twice as well as men to be thought half as good. Luckily, this is not difficult.
Charlotte Whitton

Thirty-five is when you finally get your head together and your body starts falling apart.
Caryn Leschen

I try to take one day at a time – but sometimes several days attack me at once.
Jennifer Unlimited

If you can't be a good example – then you'll just have to be a horrible warning.
Catherine

~~~

A study in the Washington Post says that women have better verbal skills than men. I just want to say to the authors of that study, "Duh."
Conan O'Brien

Relationships are hard. It's like a full time job, and we should treat it like one. If your boyfriend or girlfriend wants to leave you, they should give you two weeks' notice. There should be severance pay, the day before they leave you, they should have to find you a temp.
Bob Ettinger

Ah, yes, divorce, from the Latin word meaning to rip out a man's genitals through his wallet.
Robin Williams

Instead of getting married again, I'm going to find a woman I don't like and just give her a house.
Rod Stewart

My mother never saw the irony in calling me a son-of-a-bitch.
Jack Nicholson

The problem with political jokes is they get elected.
Henry Cate VII

We hang the petty thieves and appoint the great ones to public office.
Aesop

If we got one-tenth of what was promised to us in these acceptance speeches there wouldn't be any inducement to go to heaven.
Will Rogers

Those who are too smart to engage in politics are punished by being governed by those who are dumber.
Plato

Politicians are the same all over. They promise to build a bridge even where there is no river.
Nikita Krushchev

When I was a boy I was told that anybody could become President. I'm beginning to believe it.
Clarence Darrow

Why pay money to have your family tree traced; go into politics and your opponents will do it for you.
Author Unknown

Politicians are people who, when they see the light at the end of the tunnel, go out and buy some more tunnel.
John Quinton

Politics is the gentle art of getting votes from the poor and campaign funds from the rich, by promising to protect each from the other.
Oscar Ameringer

I offer my opponents a bargain. If they stop telling lies about us, I will stop telling the truth about them.
Adlai Stevenson, Campaign Speech 1952

A politician is a fellow who will lay down your life for his country.
Texas Guinan

Any American who is prepared to run for president should automatically, by definition, be disqualified from ever doing so.
Gore Vidal

I have come to the conclusion that politics is too serious a matter to be left to the policitians.
Charles de Gaulle

Instead of giving a politician the keys to the city, it might be better to change the locks.
Doug Larson

The important thing is to not stop questioning. Curiosity has its own reason for existing.
Albert Einstein

George Carlin's New Rules

New Rule: No more gift registries. You know, it used to be just for weddings. Now it's for babies and new homes and graduations from rehab. Picking out the stuff you want and having other people buy it for you isn't gift giving, it's the white people's version of looting.

New Rule: Stop giving me that pop-up ad for classmates.com ! There's a reason you don't talk to people for 25 years; it's because you don't particularly like them! Besides, I already know what the captain of the football team is doing these days --- mowing my lawn.

New Rule: Don't eat anything that's served to you out a window unless you're a seagull. People are acting all shocked that a human finger was found in a bowl of Wendy's chili. Hey, it cost less than a dollar. What did you expect it to contain? Lobster?

New Rule: Stop saying that teenage boys who have sex with their hot, blonde teachers are permanently damaged . I have a better description for these kids: 'Lucky bastards.'

New Rule: Ladies, leave your eyebrows alone. Here's how much men care about your eyebrows: Do you have two of them? Good, we're done.

New Rule: There's no such thing as flavored water. There's a whole aisle of this crap at the supermarket - water, but without that 'watery' taste. Sorry, but flavored water is called a soft drink. You want flavored water? Pour some scotch over ice and let it melt. That's your flavored water.

New Rule: The more complicated the Starbucks order, the bigger the asshole. If you walk into a Starbucks and order a 'decaf grandee, half-soy, half-low fat, iced vanilla, double-shot, gingerbread cappuccino, extra dry, light ice, with one Sweet-n'-Low, and One NutraSweet,' Ooooh, you're a huge asshole.

New Rule: I'm not the cashier! By the time I look up from sliding my card, entering my PIN number, pressing 'Enter,' verifying the amount, deciding, no, I don't want Cash back, and pressing 'Enter' again, the kid who is supposed to be ringing me up is standing there eating my Mars Bar.

New Rule: Just because your tattoo has Chinese characters in it doesn't make you Spiritual. It's right above the crack of your ass. And it probably translates to 'beef with broccoli.' The last time you did anything spiritual, you were praying to God you weren't pregnant. You're not spiritual. You're just high.

New Rule: If you're going to insist on making movies based on crappy old television shows, then you have to give everyone in the Cineplex a remote so we can see what's playing on the other screens. Let's remember that the reason something was a television show in the first place is that the idea wasn't good enough to be a movie.

New Rule: And this one is long overdue: No more bathroom attendants. After I zip up, some guy is offering me a towel and a mint like I just had sex with George Michael. I can't even tell if he's supposed to be there, or just some freak with a fetish. I don't want to be on your web cam, Dude. I just want to wash my hands.

New Rule: If and when I ask how old your toddler is, I don't need to hear '27 months.' 'He's two' will do just fine. He's not a cheese. And I didn't really care in the first place.

New Rule: If you ever hope to be a credible adult and want a job that pays better than minimum wage, then for God's sake don't pierce or tattoo every available piece of flesh. If so, then plan your future around saying, 'Do you want fries with that?'

~~~

That woman speaks eighteen languages and she can't say 'No' in any of them.
Dorothy Parker

~~~

One of the greatest wise-crackers of them all was Groucho Marx. His ancestors, he was fond of saying, 'came over on the Augustflower, having missed the Mayflower'. Egged on by their mother, Minnie – who said of showbusiness, "Where else can people who don't know anything make so much money?"

"We played towns I would refuse to be buried in today," he said, "even if the funeral were free and they tossed in a tombstone." Groucho's flippancies were, on his own admission, 'oft-repeated' – in letters, on screen, in articles and interviews, and no doubt before, during and after dinner.

A man's only as old as the woman he feels.

Time wounds all heels.

Marriage is a wonderful institution...but who wants to live in an institution?

Will you marry me? Do you have any money? Answer the second question first.

I've been around so long, I knew Doris Day before she was a virgin.

Behind every successful man there is a woman, behind her is his wife.
Groucho Marx

~~~

You know you're a redneck if your home has wheels and your car doesn't.
Jeff Foxworthy

When a man opens a car door for his wife, it's either a new car or a new wife.
Prince Philip

A computer once beat me at chess, but it was no match for me at kickboxing.
Emo Philips

Wood burns faster when you have to cut and chop it yourself.
Harrison Ford

The best cure for sea sickness, is to sit under a tree.
Spike Milligan

Lawyers believe a man is innocent until proven broke.
Robin Hall

Kill one man and you're a murderer, kill a million and you're a conqueror.
Jean Rostand

Having more money doesn't make you happier. I have 50 million dollars but I'm just as happy as when I had 48 million.
Arnold Schwarzenegger

In hotel rooms I worry. I can't be the only guy who sits on the furniture naked.
Jonathan Katz

If life were fair Elvis would still be alive today and all the impersonators would be dead.
Johnny Carson

I don't believe in astrology. I am a Sagittarius and we're very skeptical.
Arthur C. Clarke

~~~

I am reminded of a joke: what happens if a politician drowns in a river? It is pollution.

What happens if all of them drown?
That is solution!

~~~

In my many years I have come to the conclusion that one useless man is a shame, two is a lawfirm, and three or more is a congress.
John Adams

If you don't read the newspaper you are uninformed, if you do read the newspaper you are misinformed.
Mark Twain

I contend that for a nation to try to tax itself into prosperity is like a man standing in a bucket and trying to lift himself up by the handle.
Winston Churchill

A government which robs Peter to pay Paul can always depend on the support of Paul.
George Bernard Shaw

A liberal is someone who feels a great debt to his fellow man, which debt
he proposes to pay off with your money.
G. Gordon Liddy

Democracy must be something more than two wolves and a sheep
voting on what to have for dinner.
James Bovard

Foreign aid might be defined as a transfer of money from poor people in
rich countries to rich people in poor countries.
Douglas Case

Giving money and powers to government is like giving whiskey and car
keys to teenage boys.
P.J. O'Rourke

Government is the great fiction, through which everybody endeavors to
live at the expense of everybody else.
Frederic Bastiat

I don't make jokes. I just watch the government and report facts.
Will Rogers

If you think healthcare is expensive now, wait until you see what it costs
when it's free!
P.J. O'Rourke

In general, the art of government consists of taking as much money as
possible from one party of the citizens to give to the other.
Voltaire (1764)

Just because you do not take an interest in politics doesn't mean politics
won't take an interest in you!
Pericles (430 B.C.)

No man's life, liberty, or property is safe while the legislature is in
session.
Mark Twain (1866)

Talk is cheap, except when Congress does it.
Anonymous

The inherent vice of capitalism is the unequal sharing of blessings. The inherent blessing of socialism is the equal sharing of misery.
Winston Churchill

The only difference between a tax man and a taxidermist is that the taxidermist leaves the skin.
Mark Twain

The ultimate result of shielding men from the effects of folly is to fill the world with fools.
Herbert Spencer, English Philosopher (1820 – 1903)

There is no distinctly Native American criminal class, save Congress.
Mark Twain

What this country needs are more unemployed politicians.
Edward Langley, Artist (1928 – 1995)

A government big enough to give you everything you want, is strong enough to take everything you have.
Thomas Jefferson

Until I was thirteen, I thought my name was Shut Up.
Joe Namath

You know 'that look' women get when they want sex? My neither.
Steve Martin

May your troubles be less, may your blessings be more and may nothing but happiness come through your door.
Unknown

Be careful about reading health books. You might die of a misprint.
Mark Twain

Having sex is like playing bridge. If you don't have a good partner, you'd better have a good hand.
Woody Allen

Last week, I stated this woman was the ugliest woman I had ever seen. I have since been visited by her sister, and now wish to withdraw that statement.
Mark Twain

I had a rose named after me and I was very flattered. But I was not pleased to read the description in the catalogue, 'No good in a bed, but fine against a wall.'
Eleanor Roosevelt

According to a new survey, women say they feel more comfortable undressing in front of men than they do undressing in front of other women. They say that women are too judgmental, where, of course, men are just grateful.
Robert De Niro

The only reason they say 'women and children first' is to test the strength of the lifeboats.
Jean Kerr

I've been married to a communist and a fascist, and neither would take out the garbage.
Zsa Zsa Gabor

See, the problem is that God gives men a brain and a penis, and only enough blood to run one at a time.
Robin Williams

When the white missionaries came to Africa they had the Bible and we had the land. They said, 'let us pray.' We closed our eyes. When we opened them we had the Bible and they had the land.
Desmond Tutu

Sex at age 90 is like trying to shoot pool with a rope.
George Burns

America is the only country where a significant proportion of the population believes that professional wrestling is real but the moon landing was faked.
David Letterman

I'm not a paranoid, deranged millionaire. God dammit, I'm a billionaire.
Howard Hughes

Men are like linoleum floors. Lay 'em right and you can walk all over them for thirty years.
Betsy Salkind

YOGI BERRA QUOTES

To Billy Martin who had locked his keys in his car, "You gotta call a blacksmith."

About golf, "Ninety percent of the putts that fall short don't go in."

On the 1973 pennant race, "It ain't over until it's over."

To a fellow Yankee who said he was waiting for Bo Derek, "Well, I haven't seen him."

Asked what he does on the afternoon of a night game, "I take a two-hour nap, from one o'clock to four."

His overall baseball philosophy, "Ninety percent of this game is half mental."

About a popular Minneapolis restaurant, "Nobody goes there anymore, it's too crowded."

Explaining why it's tough to play in Yankee Stadium on a fall afternoon, "It gets late early out there."

To Joe Altobelli on his 50th birthday, "Now you're an old Italian scallion."

When he was honored in St. Louis, "I want to thank all those who made this night necessary."

If you don't know where you are going, you might end up someplace else.

~~~

I didn't attend the funeral, but I sent a nice letter saying I approved of it.
Mark Twain

He has no enemies, but is intensely disliked by his friends.
Oscar Wilde

I am enclosing two tickets to the first night of my new play, bring a friend...if you have one.
George Bernard Shaw to Winston Churchill

Cannot possibly attend first night, will attend second, if there is one."
Winston Churchill

I feel so miserable without you; it's almost like having you here.
Stephen Bishop

He is a self-made man and worships his creator.
John Bright

I've just learned about his illness. Let's hope it's nothing trivial.
Irvin S. Cobb

He is not only dull himself, he is the cause of dullness in others.
Samuel Johnson

He is simply a shiver looking for a spine to run up.
Paul Keating

There's nothing wrong with you that reincarnation won't cure.
Jack E. Leonard

He has the attention span of a lightning bolt.
Robert Redford

They never open their mouths without subtracting from the sum of human knowledge.
Thomas Brackett Reed

In order to avoid being called a flirt, she always yielded easily.
Charles Count Talleyrand

He loves nature in spite of what it did to him.
Forrest Tucker

Why do you sit there looking like an envelope without any address on it?
Mark Twain

His mother should have thrown him away and kept the stork.
Mae West

Some cause happiness wherever they go; others, whenever they go.
Oscar Wilde

He uses statistics as a drunken man uses lamp-posts....for support rather than illumination.
Andrew Lang (1844 – 1912)

He is Van Gogh's ear for music.
Billy Wilder

I've had a perfectly wonderful evening. But this wasn't it.
Groucho Marx

I never drink water becaues of the disgusting things that fish do in it.
W.C. Fields

Bisexuality immediately doubles your chances for a date on Saturday night.
Rodney Dangerfield

Sometimes, when I look at my children, I say to myself, "Lillian, you should have remained a virgin."
Lillian Carter (mother of Jimmy Carter)

Maybe it's true that life begins at fifty, but everything else starts to wear out, fall out, and spread out.
Phyllis Diller

I have never hated a man enough to give his diamonds back.
Zsa Zsa Gabor

My girlfriend always laughs during sex – no matter what she's reading.
Steve Jobs

Mercy to the guilty is cruelty to the innocent.
Adam Smith

MAYE WEST QUOTES

I always keep a diary, and some day it will keep you.

One man in the house is worth two in the street.

When you think about it, what other playwrights are there besides
O'Neill, Tennessee and me?

I used to be Snow White, but I drifted.

~~~

By the time a man is wise enough to watch his step, he's too old to go
anywhere.
Billy Crystal

Don't worry about avoiding temptation. As you grow older, it will avoid
you.
Winston Churchill

And the cardiologist's diet – if it tastes good, spit it out.

Only Irish coffee provides in a single glass all four essential food groups:
alcohol, caffeine, sugar and fat.
Alex Levine

I believe that sex is one of the most beautiful, natural, wholesome things
that money can buy.
Tom Clancy

Money can't buy you happiness…but it does bring you a more pleasant
form of misery.
Spike Milligan

We could certainly slow the aging process down if it had to work its way
through Congress.
Will Rogers

Santa Clause has the right idea. Visit people only once a year.
Victor Borge

Hollywood must be the only place on earth where you can be fired by a
man wearing a Hawaiian shirt and a baseball cap.
Steve Martin

Home cooking. Where many a man thinks his wife is.
Jimmy Durante

Phyllis Diller Quotes

Most children threaten at times to run away from home. This is the only thing that keeps some parents going.

We spend the first twelve months of our children's lives teaching them to walk and talk and the next twelve telling them to sit down and shut up.

I asked the waiter, "Is the milk fresh?" He said, "Lady, three hours ago it was grass."

The reason women don't play football is because 11 of them could never wear the same outfit in public.

My mother-in-law had a pain beneath her left breast. Turned out to be a trick knee.

Whatever you may look like, marry a man your own age. As your beauty fades, so will his eyesight.

A bachelor is a guy who never made the same mistake once.

A smile is a curve that sets everything straight.

Cleaning your house while your kids are still growing up is like shoveling the walk before is stops snowing.

I'm eighteen years behind in my ironing.

You know you're old if your walker has an airbag.

What I don't like about office Christmas parties is looking for a job the next day.

Burt Reynolds once asked me out. I was in his room.

I want my children to have all the things I couldn't afford. Then I want to move in with them.

~~~

As I hurtled through space, one thought kept crossing my mind – every part of this rocket was supplied by the lowest bidder.
John Glenn

America is so advanced that even the chairs are electric.
Doug Hamwell

The first piece of luggage on the carousel never belongs to anyone
George Roberts

Women need a reason to have sex. Men just need a place.
Billy Crystal

If toast always lands butter-side down, and cats always land on their feet, what happens if you strap toast on the back of a cat?
Steven Wright

If God had intended us to fly he would have made it easier to get to the airport.
Jonathan Winters

To a smart girl men are no problem – they're the answer
Zsa Zsa Gabor

I'm an excellent housekeeper. Every time I get divorced, I keep the house.
Zsa Zsa Gabor

RAISING CHILDREN

KIDS IN CHURCH

Three-year-old Reese, "Our Father, who does are in heaven, Harold is His name, Amen."

A little boy was overheard praying, "Lord, if you can't make me a better boy, don't worry about it, I'm having a real good time like I am."

You know your kids have grown up when...
Your daughter begins to put on lipstick...
Or when your son starts to wipe it off.

How come it takes so little time for a child who is afraid of the dark to become a teenager who wants to stay out all night?

WHY WE LOVE CHILDREN

A kindergarten pupil told his teacher he'd found a cat, but it was dead. "How do you know that the cat was dead?" she asked him.

"Because I pissed in its ear and it didn't move," answered the child innocently.

"You did what??!!" the teacher exclaimed in surprise.

"You know," exclaimed the boy, "I leaned over and went, 'Pssst!' and it didn't move."

~~~

A little girl goes to the barber shop with her father. She stands next to the barber chair, while her dad gets his hair cut, eating a snack cake. The barber says to her, "Sweetheart, you're gonna get hair on your Twinkie."

She says, "Yes, I know, and I'm gonna get boobs, too."

~~~

A small boy is sent to bed by his father. Five minutes later, "Da-aaad!"

"What?"

"I'm thirsty. Can you bring me a drink of water?"

"No, you had your chance. Lights out."

Five minutes later, "Da-aaad!"

"What?!"

"I'm thirsty! Can I have a drink of water?"

"I told you no! If you ask again, I'll have to spank you!"

Five minutes later, "Daaaa-aaaaa! When you come to spank me, can you bring a drink of water?"

~~~

An exasperated mother, whose son was always getting into mischief, finally asked him, "How do you expect to get into Heaven?"

The boy thought it over and said, "Well, I'll run in and out and in and out and keep slaming the door until St. Peter says, 'For Heaven's sake, Dylan, some in or stay out!'"

~~~

One summer evening during a violent thunderstorm a mother was tucking her son into bed. She was about to turn off the light when he asked with a tremor in his voice, "Mommy, will you sleep with me tonight?"

The mother smiled and gave him a reassuring hug. "I can't dear," she said, "I have to sleep in Daddy's room." A long silence was broken at last by his shaky little voice, "The big sissy."

~~~

When I was six months pregnant with my third child, my three-year-old came into the room as I was preparing to get into the shower. She said, "Mommy, you are getting fat!"

I replied, "Yes, honey, remember Mommy has a baby growing in her tummy."

"I know," she replied, "but what's growing in your butt?"

~~~

One day the first grade teacher was reading the story of Chicken Little to her class. She came to the part where Chicken Little warns the farmer. She read, "...and Chicken Little went up to the farmer and said, 'the sky is falling!'" The teacher then asked the class, "And what do you think that farmer said?" One little girl raised her hand and said, "I think he said, "Holy Sh*t! A talking chicken!"

The teacher was unable to teach for the next ten minutes.

TWO LITTLE BOYS

Two little boys, ages 8 and 10, are excessively mischievous. They are always getting into trouble and their parents know if any mischief occurs in their town, the two boys are probably involved.

The boys' mother heard that a preacher in town had been successful in disciplining children, so she asked if he would speak with her boys. The preacher agreed, but he asked to see them individually.

The mother sent the eight-year-old in the morning, with the older boy to see the preacher in the afternoon.

The preacher, a huge man with a deep booming voice, sat the younger boy down and asked him sternly, "Do you know where God is, son?"

The boy's mouth dropped open, but he made no response, sitting there wide-eyed with his mouth hanging open.

So the preacher repeated the question in an even sterner tone, "Where is God?!"

Again, the boy made no attempt to answer.

The preacher raised his voice even more and shook his finger in the boy's face and bellowed, "Where is God?!"

The boy screamed and bolted from the room, ran directly home and dove into his closet, slamming the door behind him.

When his older brother found him in the closet, he asked "What happened?"

The younger brother, gasping for breath, replied, "We are in BIG trouble this time!"

"GOD is missing, and they think WE did it!"

~~~

After the Christening of his baby brother in church, Jason sobbed all the way home in the back seat of the car. His father asked him three times what was wrong. Finally, the boy replied, "That preacher said he wanted us brought up in a Christian home, and I wanted to stay with you guys."

~~~

A wife invited some people to dinner. At the table, she turned to their six-year-old daughter and said, "Would you like to say the blessing?"

I wouldn't know what to say," the girl replied."

"Just say what you hear Mommy say," the wife answered.

The daughter bowed her head and said, "Lord, why on earth did I invite all these people to dinner?"

SHOW AND TELL

A kindergarten teacher gave her class a "show and tell" assignment. Each student was instructed to bring in an object that represented their religion to share with the class.

The first student got up in front of the class and said, "My name is Benjamin and I am Jewish and this is a Star of David."

The second student got up in front of the class and said, "My name is Mary. I'm a Catholic and this is a Rosary."

The third student got up in front of the class and said, "My name is Tommy. I am Methodist, and this is a casserole."

Goat For Dinner

The young couple invited their elderly pastor for Sunday dinner. While they were in the kitchen preparing for the meal, the minister asked their son what they were having.

"Goat," the little boy replied.

"Goat?" replied the startled man of the cloth, "Are you sure about that?"

"Yep," said the youngster, "I heard dad say to mom, 'Today is just as good as any to have the old goat for dinner."

~~~

A father was at the beach with his children when the four-year-old son ran up to him, grabbed his hand, and led him to the sand. "Daddy, what happened to him?" the son asked.

"He died and went to Heaven," the dad replied.

The boy thought for a moment and then said, "Did God throw him back down?"

~~~

A mother was preparing pancakes for her sons, Kevin, aged five, and Ryan, aged three. The boys began to argue over who would get the first pancake. Their mother saw the opportunity for a moral lesson. "If Jesus were sitting here, He would say, 'Let my brother have the first pancake, I can wait.'"

Kevin turned to his younger brother and said, "Ryan, you be Jesus!"

~~~

What did Adam say to Eve on the day before Christmas?
It's Christmas, Eve!

Quips, Quotes, Zingers & One Liners
283

~~~

A boy was doing his geography homework one evening when he turned to his father and asked, "Dad, where are the Andes?"

"Don't ask me," said the father, "Ask your mother. She puts everything away in this house."

~~~

Little Johnny's father was disappointed that the boy scored such low marks in a school spelling test. "Why did you get such a bad mark?" he asked.

"Absence," said Little Johnny.

"What do you mean? Were you absent on the day of the test?"

"No," said Little Johnny, "but the boy who sits next to me was!"

~~~

Little Johhny's father said, "Can I see your school report?"

"I haven't got it," said Johnny.

"Why not?"

"My friend Kenny borrowed it. He wants to scare his parents."

~~~

The teacher called Little Johnny to her desk. She told him, "This essay you've written about your pet dog is word for word exactly the same essay as your brother has written."

"Of course it is," said Johnny, "It's the same dog!"

~~~

Arriving home from school, Little Johnny told his mother, "My teacher thinks I'm going to be famous."

"Really?" said his mother. "Why? What did she say?"

"She said all I have to do is mess up one more time and I'm history!"

~~~

To My Children

When I spill some food on my nice clean dress
Or maybe forget to tie my shoe,
Please be patient and perhaps reminisce
About the many hours I spent with you.

When I taught you how to eat with care,
Plus tying laces and your numbers, too,
Dressing yourself and combing your hair,
Those were precious hours spent with you.

So when I forget what I was about to say,
Just give me a minute - or maybe two.
It probably wasn't important anyway,
And I would much rather listen just to you.

If I tell the story one more time,
And you know the ending through and through,
Please remember your first nursery rhyme
When I rehearsed it a hundred times with you.

When my legs are tired and it's hard to stand
Or walk the steady pace that I would like to do,
Please take me carefully by my hand,
And guide me now as I so often did for you.

~~~

A man in a hurry taking his eight-year-old son to school made a right turn at a red light.

"Uh-oh!" he said. "I think I just made an illegal turn."

"It's okay, Dad," said the boy. "The police car right behind us did the same thing."

It was that time, during the Sunday morning service, for the children's sermon. All the children were invited to come forward. One little girl was wearing a particularly pretty dress and, as she sat down, the minister leaned over and said, "That is a very pretty dress. Is it your Easter dress?"

The little girl replied, directly into the minister's clip-on microphone, "Yes, and my mum says it's a bitch to iron."

~~~

A certain little girl, when asked her name, would reply, "I'm Mr. Sugarbrown's daughter."

Her mother told her this was wrong, she must say, "I'm Jane Sugarbrown."

The Vicar spoke to her in Sunday School, and said, "Aren't you Mr. Sugarbrown's daughter?"

She replied, "I thought I was, but mother says I'm not."

~~~

A little girl asked her mother, "Can I go outside and play with the boys?"

Her mother replied, "No, you can't play with the boys, they're too rough."

The little girl thought about if for a few moments and asked, "If I can find a smooth one, can I play with him?"

~~~

A little boy was doing his math homework. He said to himself, "Two plus five, that son of a bitch is seven. Three plus six, that son of a bitch is nine..."

His mother heard what he was saying and gasped, "What are you doing?"

The little boy answered, "I'm doing my math homework, Mum."

"And this is how your teacher taught you to do it?" the mother asked.

"Yes," he answered.

Infuriated, the mother asked the teacher the next day, "What are you teaching my son in math?"

The teacher replied, "Right now, we are learning addition."

The mother asked, "And are you teaching them to say two plus two, that son of a bitch is four?"

After the teacher stopped laughing, she answered, "What I taught them was, two plus two, THE SUM OF WHICH, is four."

~~~

I CHILDPROOFED MY HOUSE BUT THEY STILL GET IN.

LITTLE BRUCE AND JENNY

Little Bruce and Jenny are only ten years old, but they just know that they are in love. One day they decide that they want to get married, so Bruce goes to Jenny's father to ask him for her hand.

Bruce bravely walks up to him and says, "Mr. Smith, me and Jenny are in love and I want to ask you for her hand in marriage."

Thinking that this was just the cutest thing, Mr. Smith replies, "Well Bruce, you are only ten. Where will you two live?"

Without even taking a moment to think about it, Bruce replies "In Jenny's room. It's bigger than mine and we can both fit there nicely."

Still thinking this is just adorable, Mr. Smith says with a huge grin, "Okay then how will you live? You're not old enough to get a job. You'll need to support Jenny."

Again, Bruce instantly replies, "Our allowance. Jenny makes five bucks a week and I make 10 bucks a week. That's about 60 bucks a month and that should do us just fine."

By this time Mr. Smith is a little shocked that Bruce has put so much thought into this. He thinks for a moment trying to come up with something that Bruce won't have an answer to.

After a second, Mr. Smith says, "Well Bruce, it seems like you have got everything all figured out. I just have one more question for you. What will you do if the two of you should have little ones of your own?"

Bruce just shrugs his shoulders and says, "Well, we've been lucky so far."

Mr. Smith no longer thinks the twit is adorable.

~~~

Johhny asked his grandma how old she was. Grandma answered, "Thirty-nine and holding."

Johnny thought for a moment and then said, "How old would you be if you let go?"

~~~

These are actual comments made on students' report cards by teachers in the New York City public school system. All teachers were reprimanded, but, boy, are these funny!!

1)   Since my last report, your child has reached rock bottom and has started to dig.

2)   I would not allow this student to breed.

3)   Your child has delusions of adequacy.

4) Your son is depriving a village somewhere of an idiot.

5) Your son sets low personal standards and then consistently fails to achieve them.

6) The student has a 'full six-pack' but lacks the plastic thing to hold it all together.

7) This child has been working with glue too much.

8) When your daughter's IQ reaches 50, she should sell.

9) The gates are down, the lights are flashing, but the train isn't coming.

10) If this student were any more stupid, he'd have to be watered twice a week.

11) It's impossible to believe the sperm that created this child beat out 1,000,000 others.

12) The wheel is turning but the hamster is definitely dead.

~~~

Being considerate of others will take your children further in life than any college degree.
Marian Wright Edelman

~~~

The country clubs, the cars, the boats,
Your assets may be ample,
But the best inheritance
You can leave your kids
Is to be a good example.
Barry Spilchuk

~~~

A mother, exasperated with her four year old not doing what he was told, finally shouted, "David, how many times must I tell you?"

His response, with a puzzled look on his face, "Four?"

REALITY

The defendant stood defiantly in the dock and said to the judge, "I don't recognize this court."

"Why?" barked the judge.

"Because you've had it decorated since the last time I was here."

~~~

A man said to his friends, "I went to the dentist this morning."

"So does your tooth still hurt?" asked the friend.

"I don't know. He kept it."

~~~

Banging your head against a wall uses 150 calories an hour.
(Who volunteers for these tests?)

Humans and dolphins are the only species that have sex for pleasure.
(Is that why Flipper was always smiling?)

The ant can lift 50 times its own weight, can pull 30 times its own weight and always falls over on its right side when intoxicated.
(From drinking little bottles of???)
(Did our government pay for this research?)

Butterflies taste with their feet.
(Ah, geez.)

An ostrich's eye is bigger than its brain.
(I know some people like that.)

Starfish don't have brains.
(I know some people like that too.)

Turtles can breathe through their butts.
(And I thought I had bad breath in the morning!)

~~~

I COOK USING THE FOUR FOOD GROUPS: CANNED, BOXED, BAGGED AND FROZEN

~~~

Eve was created because God was concerned that if Adam got lost in the Garden of Eden, he wouldn't ask for directions.

~~~

The judge looked at the defendant and asked, "What exactly is it you're charged with?"

"Doing my Christmas shopping early," replied the defendant.

"That's not an offence," said the judge. "How early were you doing this shopping?"

The defendant bowed his head and said, "Before the store opened."

~~~

An elderly man went to a train station booking office and said, "I'd like a return ticket, please."

"Where to?" said the clerk.

"Back to here, of course," said the old man.

~~~

On a baking hot summer's day, the temperature in the open plan office was nudging ninety degrees and the foul stench of perspiration was coming from one desk in the corner.

Eventually, one of the workers said pointedly, "Obviously, someone's deodorant isn't working."

The guy at the desk in the corner called back, "Well, it can't be me because I'm not wearing any."

~~~

At the airport check-in desk, a woman passenger told the clerk, "I want you to send one of my bags to New York, one to Chicago and the other one to Los Angeles."

"Sorry, we can't do that," said the clerk.

The woman snapped, "Well, you did last week!"

~~~

A woman was driving along the road when the car in front braked suddenly and she ploughed into the back of it.

When the driver got out, the woman saw that he was short in stature. He said, "I'm not happy."

The woman said, "Well, which one are you?"

~~~

The soul always knows what to do to heal itself.
The challenge is to silence the mind.

~~~

A man got lost and called in to a village shop to ask for directions. He asked the shopkeeper, "Can you tell me the quickest way to Bristol?"

"Are you walking or driving?" asked the shopkeeper.

"Driving."

"Good, because that's definitely the quickest way."

~~~

A customer in a restaurant asked, "How do you prepare the chicken?"

"We don't," said the waiter, "We just tell it straight that it's going to die."

LETTER TO THE EDITOR

I find it extremely irritating to be reading the Sun and be distracted by obvious spelling mistakes. You have contributors and columnists who seem to think that cars 'break' at stop signs, (although with drivers in Toronto, this too is a possibility), books have 'forwards' (apparently they haven't read any books); can't tell the difference between 'wrack' and 'rack' (although he might be pain-wracked if put on a rack); think that we park cars at parking 'metres' (metres are a unit of measurement, and meters are used to measure something); obviously have not seen the word 'ado' in a sentence, or wouldn't have written 'much adieu about nothing;' the list goes on and on. I know the educational system has become a joke in Ontario, but to keep people who don't know English well enough to spell words properly in context employed as 'journalists' is a bigger joke. Where are the 'editors' who are supposed to be 'editing' this stuff before publication? Do you just send this stuff directly from the writers' computers to the presses without review? I generally enjoy the Sun and its style of reporting, yet I cannot understand how you can publish an 'English-language' daily in which English is quite obviously a second language.

Barry Levy

You don't say when these mistakes where made. How do we no you're write?"

~~~

Yuckitty-Yuck: After a two-year study, the U.S. National Science Foundation has announced the results of a study on corporate America's recreation preferences.

The sport of choice for maintenance level employees is bowling. For supervisors, it is baseball.

The favourite sport for middle management is tennis, and for corporate officers it is golf.

Conclusion: The higher you are in the corporate structure, the smaller your balls – scientifically speaking, of course.

~~~

A chicken and a pig were drinking together in a bar one evening when the chicken said, "Why don't we go into business together? We could open a ham and egg restaurant."

"Not so fast," said the pig, "For you, it's just a day's work. For me, it's a matter of life and death."

~~~

A man sitting in a bar asked the bartender, "How late does the band play?"

The bartender replied, "About a half-beat behind the drummer."

~~~

You can fool some of the people all the time, but you can't fool mom!

MONEY TALKS…
MINE KEEPS SAYING GOODBYE.

Warning, I have an attitude and I know how to use it.

If things get better with age, then I am positively magnificent.

I'm so far behind, I think I'm first.

Next mood swing in five minutes

PUT YOUR BIG GIRL PANTIES ON AND DEAL WITH IT!

When did my wild oats become shredded wheat?

You call it grey hair, I call it stress highlights!

I finally got my head together, now my body is falling apart.

Bring coffee and no one gets hurt!

DOMESTICALLY CHALLENGED!

The way to a woman's heart is through the door of a good restaurant.

The government has found a new way to save its money. It uses mine.

You know your spouse is getting plenty tired of you when she wraps your lunch in a roadmap.

Patient: I feel schizophrenic.
Psychologist: Well, that makes four of us.

Quips, Quotes, Zingers & One Liners

I used to cut class from correspondence school by sending in empty envelopes.

Men and women can fail many times, but they aren't failures until they begin to blame someone else.

Ruth: My husband was named Man of the Year.
Betty: Well, that shows you what kind of a year it was.

Psychiatrist: Now tell me about this dream you had.
Patient: Well, I had a dream I was walking down the street with nothing on but a hat.
Psychiatrist: And you were embarrassed?
Patient: You bet I was. It was last year's hat.

Effiency experts are smart enough to tell you how to run your own business, and too smart to start their own.

~~~

"It is my deep hope that the people of the world will be able to separate 'America' from 'Americans' and know how sorry, remorseful, ashamed and disgusted the vast majority of Americans are – both in regards to this war and that in Iraq. We want peace, but just like elsewhere, we are largely powerless over the actions of our government."
Joshua, Tucson AZ

~~~

Mid-life is when you go to the doctor and you realize you are now so old, you have to pay someone to look at you naked...

HOW TO STAY YOUNG
BY GEORGE CARLIN

1) Throw out nonessential numbers. This includes age, weight and height. Let the doctor worry about them. That is why you pay him/her.

2) Keep only cheerful friends. The grouches pull you down.

3) Keep learning. Learn more about the computer, crafts, gardening, whatever. Never let the brain idle. "An idle mind is the devil's workshop." And the devil's name is Alzheimer's.

4) Enjoy the simple things.

5) Laugh often, long and loud. Laugh until you gasp for breath.

6) The tears happen. Endure, grieve, and move on. The only person who is with us our entire life, is ourselves. Be ALIVE while you are alive.

7) Surround yourself with what you love, whether it's family, pets, keepsakes, music, plants, hobbies, whatever. Your home is your refuge.

8) Cherish your health: If it is good, preserve it. If it is unstable, improve it. If it is beyond what you can improve, get help.

9) Don't take guilt trips. Take a trip to the mall, to the next county, to a foreign country, but NOT to where the guilt is.

10) Tell the people you love that you love them, at every opportunity.

BLIND DATE

"How was your blind date?" a college student asked her roommate.

"Terrible!" the roommate answered. "He showed up in his 1932 Rolls Royce."

"Wow, that's a very expensive car. What's so bad about that?"

To which she replied, "He was the original owner."

~~~

LAUGH A LITTLE EACH DAY.
IT'S BETTER THAN CHICKEN SOUP.
AT LEAST THAT'S WHAT THE CHICKENS SAY.

The Importance of Walking

Walking can add minutes to your life.
This enables you at 85 years old to spend an additional five months in a nursing home.

~~~

Now that I'm older, I thought it was great that I seemed to have more patience. Turns out that I just don't give a shit.

What I Want In A Man (Original List)

1) Handsome
2) Charming
3) Financially successful
4) A caring listener
5) Witty
6) In good shape
7) Dresses with style
8) Appreciates finer things
9) Full of thoughtful surprises

What I Want In A Man (Age 32)

1) Nice looking
2) Open's car doors, holds chairs
3) Has enough money for a nice dinner
4) Listens more than talks
5) Laughs at my jokes
6) Carries bags of groceries with ease
7) Owns at least one tie
8) Appreciates a good home-cooked meal
9) Remember's birthday's and anniversaries

What I Want In A Man (Age 42)

1) Not too ugly
2) Doesn't drive off until I'm in the car
3) Works steady – splurges on dinner out occassionally

4) Nods head when I'm talking
5) Usualy remembers punch lines of jokes
6) Is in good enough shape to rearrange the furniture
7) Wears a shirt that covers his stomach
8) Knows not to buy champagne with screwtop lids
9) Remembers to put the toilet seat down
10) Shaves most weekends

WHAT I WANT IN A MAN (AGE 52)

1) Keeps hair in nose and ears trimmed
2) Doesn't belch or scratch in public
3) Doesn't borrow money too often
4) Doesn't nod off to sleep when I'm venting
5) Doesn't re-tell the same joke too many times
6) Is in good enough shape to get off the couch on weekends
7) Usually wears matching socks and fresh underwear
8) Appreciates a good TV dinner
9) Remembers your name on occasion
10) Shaves some weekends

WHAT I WANT IN A MAN (AGE 62)

1) Doesn't scare small children
2) Remembers where bathroom is
3) Doesn't require much money for upkeep
4) Only snores lightly when asleep
5) Remembers why he's laughing
6) Is in good enough shape to stand up by himself
7) Usually wears some clothes
8) Likes soft foods
9) Remembers where he left his teeth
10) Remembers that it is the weekend

WHAT I WANT IN A MAN (AGE 72)

1) Breathing
2) Doesn't miss the toilet

WALMART APPLICANT

Below is an actual job application that this 75 year old senior citizen submitted to Walmart in California. They hired him because he was funny.

NAME: Kenneth Way (Grumpy Old Bastard)
SEX: Not lately, but I am looking for the right woman (or at least one who will cooperate)
DESIRED POSITION: Company President or Vice President. But seriously, whatever's available. If I was in a position to be picky, I wouldn't be applying here in the first place.
DESIRED SALARY: $185,000 a year plus stock options and a Michael Orvitz style severance package. If that's not possible, make an offer and we can haggle.
EDUCATION: Yes
LAST POSITION HELD: Target for middle management hostility.
PREVIOUS SALARY: A lot less than I'm worth
MOST NOTABLE ACHIEVEMENT: My incredible collection of stolen pens and post-it notes
REASON FOR LEAVING: It sucked
HOURS AVAILABLE TO WORK: Any
PREFERRED HOURS: 1:30 – 3:30 p.m., Monday, Tuesday, and Thursday

~~~

A group of 40-year-old buddies discuss and discuss where they should meet for dinner. Finally, it is agreed upon that they should meet at the Gausthof zum Lowen restaurant because the waitresses there have low cut blouses and nice breasts.

10 years later, at 50 years of age, the group meets and once again they discuss and discuss where they should eat. Finally, it is agreed upon that they should meet at the Gausthof zum Lowen because the food there is very good and the wine selection is good also.

10 years later, at 60 years of age, the group meets and once again they discuss and discuss where they should eat. Finally, it is agreed upon that they should meet at the Gausthof zum Lowen because they can eat there in peace and quiet and the restaurant is smoke free.

10 years later, at 70 years of age, the group meets and once again they discuss and discuss where they should eat. Finally, it is agreed upon that they should meet at the Gausthof zum Lowen because the restaurant is wheelchair accessible and they even have an elevator.

10 years later, at 80 years of age, the group meets and once again they discuss and discuss where they should eat. Finally, it is agreed upon that they should meet at the Gausthof zum Lowen because that would be a great idea as they have never been there before.

~~~

An elderly gent was invited to an old friends home for dinner one evening. He was impressed by the way his buddy preceded every request to his wife with endearing terms, such as Honey, My Love, Darling, Sweeheart, Pumpkin, etcetera. The couple had been married almost 70 years and, clearly, they were still very much in love.

While the wife was in the kitchen, the man leaned over to his host, "I think it's wonderful that, after all these years, you still call your wife those loving pet names."

The old man hung his head, "I have to tell you the truth," he said, "Her name slipped my mind about 10 years ago, and I'm scared to death to ask the cranky old bitch what her name is."

COUNTRY PREACHER AND HIS TEENAGE SON

An old country preacher had a teenage son, and it was getting time the boy should give some thought along the line of choosing a profession. Like many young men, then and now, the boy didn't really know what he wanted to do - and he didn't seem overly concerned about it.

One day, while the boy was away at school, his father decided to try an experiment. What he did was, he went into the boy's room and placed on his study table these four objects: a Bible, a silver dollar, a bottle of whiskey and a Playboy magazine

"I'll just hide behind the door here," the old preacher said to himself. "When my son comes home from school today, I'll see which of these four objects he picks up.

Quips, Quotes, Zingers & One Liners
303

If he picks up the Bible, he's going to be a preacher like me, and what a Blessing that would be!

If he picks up the dollar, he's going to be a businessman, and that would be okay too.

But if he picks up the bottle, he's going to be a no-good bum, and Lord, what a shame that would be."

"And worst of all, if he picks up that magazine, he's going to be a skirt-chasing womanizer."

The old man waited anxiously, and soon he heard his son's footsteps as he entered the house whistling and headed for his room.

The boy tossed his books on the bed, and as he turned around to leave the room he spotted the objects on the table.

With curiousity in his eye, he walked over to inspect them. Finally, he picked up the Bible and placed it under his arm. He picked up the silver dollar and dropped it into his pocket. He uncorked the bottle and took a big drink while he admired this month's centerfold.

"Lord have mercy," the old preacher whispered, "He's gonna be a politician!"

SEX AFTER DEATH

A couple made a deal that whoever died first would come back and inform the other of the afterlife.

Their biggest fear was that there was no afterlife at all.

After a long life together, the husband was the first to die. True to his word, he made the first contact, "Marion, Marion."

"Is that you Bob?"

"Yes, I've come back like we agreed."

"That's wonderful! What's it like?"

"Well, I get up in the morning, I have sex, I have breakfast and then it's off to the golf course. I have sex again, bathe in the warm sun and then have sex a couple more times. Then I have lunch, another romp around the golf course, then pretty much have sex the rest of the afternoon. After supper, it's back to the golf course again. Then it's more sex until late at night. I catch some much needed sleep and then the next day it starts all over again."

"Oh, Bob you must be in Heaven!"

"Not exactly... I'm a rabbit on a golf course in Arizona."

IF YOU WANT BREAKFAST IN BED, SLEEP IN THE KITCHEN.

Instant Human Just add coffee

Time may be a great healer, but it's a lousy beautician.

If you think pushing 60 is hard, wait 'til you start pulling it!

I barely survived yesterday and it's today already!

WORK IS FOR THE PEOPLE WHO DON'T GOLF.

A bad day of golf beats a good day of work.

An optimist is a fisherman who takes along a camera.

A great fisherman lives here with the catch of his life.

HE CLEANS THE FISH, WHY NOT THE HOUSE.

Golf isn't just a sport, it's a way of pretending that you're getting exercise.

EAT WELL, STAY FIT, DIE ANYWAY!

By the time you can make ends meet, they move the ends.

Being 'over the hill' is much better than being under it.

I PLAN ON LIVING FOREVER. SO FAR, SO GOOD.

IMPOTENCE: Nature's way of saying, "No Hard Feelings"

RETIRED
NO JOB
NO STRESS
NO PAY

You know you're over the hill when 'Getting a little action' means your prune juice is working.

Quips, Quotes, Zingers & One Liners
305

I didn't realize when I said, "I Do" that I'd do everything!

I used to burn the candle at both ends, now I can't find the matches!

Laugh until you tinkle in your panties.

I'M NOT OVERWEIGHT, I'M UNDERTALL!

My mind not only wanders, sometimes it leaves me completely!

We've been through a lot together, and most of it was your fault!

A smile and a handshake will only get you so far, after that it's all about the boobs.

NOTICE:
The opinions of the husband are not necessarily those of the management.

My husband needs new glasses. He still doesn't see things my way!

Who are these kids and why are they calling me Mom?

THE MORE I KNOW ABOUT MEN, THE MORE I LIKE MY CAT!

DO YOU KNOW THAT AWESOME FEELING WHEN YOU GET INTO BED, FALL ASLEEP, STAY ASLEEP ALL NIGHT AND WAKE UP FEELING REFRESHED AND READY TO TAKE ON THE DAY?

YEAH, ME NEITHER!

We offer three kinds of service:
GOOD – CHEAP – FAST
You can pick any two
Good service, Cheap, won't be Fast
Good service, Fast, won't be Cheap
Fast service, Cheap, won't be Good

GOD GAVE YOU TOES AS A DEVICE FOR FINDING FURNITURE IN THE DARK.

Nothing is foolproof to a sufficiently talented fool.

If the shoe fits, get another one just like it.

FLASHLIGHT: A CASE FOR HOLDING DEAD BATTERIES.

THE THINGS THAT COME TO THOSE WHO WAIT, MAY BE THE THINGS LEFT BY THOSE WHO GOT THERE FIRST.

Those who live by the sword get shot by those who don't.

The 50-50-90 Rule: Anytime you have a 50-50 chance of getting something right, there's a 90% probability you'll get it wrong.

REDNECKS

Joe-Bob was driving a tall truck as it approached a low bridge. "Oh, no," he said, "The height of the bridge is nine foot and our truck is at least ten foot!"

"It's okay," said Billy-Joe in the passenger seat, "There's no cops around."

~~~

Billy-Bob and Bubba found three hand grenades and decided to take them to the nearest police station.

"What if one of them explodes before we get there?" asked Billy Bob.

"Don't worry about it," said Bubba, "We'll just lie and tell them we only found two."

YOU MIGHT BE A REDNECK IF...

- After the prom you drove the truck while your date hit road signs with beer bottles.
- Your house doesn't have curtains but your truck does.
- You have a rag for a gas cap.
- You call your boss, "Dude".
- You think Volvo is part of a woman's anatomy
- Jack Daniels makes your list of most admired people.
- Your sister's educational goal is to get out of high school before she gets pregnant.
- Your wife's best shoes have steel toecaps.
- Your gene pool doesn't have a deep end.
- You think Dom Perignon is a Mafia leader.
- A tornado hits your neighborhood and does half a million dollars of improvements.
- You've ever had sex in a satellite dish.
- There's a gun rack on your bicycle.

- There's a wasps' nest in your living room.
- Your richest relative buys a new house and you have to help take the wheels off.
- You think beef jerky and Moon Pies are two of the major food groups.
- You use your mailbox to hold up one end of your clothesline.
- You've ever been blacklisted from a bowling alley.
- You consider a six pack of beer and a bug zapper quality entertainment.
- Your wife's hairdo has ever been ruined by a ceiling fan.
- You've ever had to scratch your sister's name out of a message that begins, "For a good time call..."
- You consider your license plate 'personalized' because your father made it.
- You own a special baseball cap for formal occasions.
- You've ever been involved in a custody battle over a hunting dog.
- Your mom's lost at least one tooth opening a beer bottle.
- Your Christmas stocking is full of ammo.
- You had a toothpick in your mouth when your wedding pictures were taken.
- Your dog and your wallet are both on a chain.
- Your brother-in-law is also your uncle.
- You prefer to walk the excess length off your jeans rather than hem them.
- Your junior-senior prom had a daycare centre.
- Your dad walks you to school because you're in the same grade.
- You have two or more brothers named Bubba or Junior.
- Your family tree does not fork.

RETIREMENT

Q: How many days in a week?
A: 7. 6 Saturdays and 1 Sunday

Q: When is a retiree's bedtime?
A: Three hours after he falls asleep on the couch.

Q: How many retirees to change a light bulb?
A: Only one, but it might take all day.

Q: What's the biggest gripe of retirees?
A: There is not enough time to get everything done.

Q: Why don't retirees mind being called Seniors?
A: The term comes with a 10% discount.

Q: Among retirees, what is considered formal attire?
A: Tied shoes.

Q: Why do retirees count pennies?
A: They are the only ones who have the time.

Q: What is the common term for someone who enjoys work and refuses to retire?
A: NUTS!

Q: What do retirees call a long lunch?
A: Normal

Q: Why are retirees so slow to clean out the basement, attic or garbage?
A: They know that as soon as they do, one of their adult kids will want to store stuff there.

Q: What is the best way to describe retirement?
A: The never ending Coffee Break.

Q: What's the biggest advantage of going back to school as a retiree?
A: If you cut classes, no one calls your parents.

The New AARP

Yep, the heck with the ultra liberal old AARP (American Association for Retired People). I joined the new AARP. My AARP card stands for Armed And Really Pissed.

~~~

Let me get this straight. Obama's healthcare plan will be written by a committee whose Chairman says he doesn't understand it, passed by a Congress which hasn't read it, signed by a President who smokes, funded by a Treasury Chief who did not pay his taxes, overseen by a Surgeon General who is obese, and financed by a country that is nearly broke. What could possibly go wrong?

~~~

Q: Someone has told me that menopause is mentioned in the Bible. Is that true? Where can it be found?
A: Yes. Matthew 14:92: "And Mary rode Joseph's ass all the way to Egypt."

Q: How can you increase the heart rate of your 60+ year old husband.
A: Tell him you're pregnant.

Q: What can I do for these crow's feet and all these wrinkles on my face?
A: Go braless. It will usually pull them out.

THOUGHTS OF A RETIRED PERSON

- I planted some birdseed. A bird came up. Now I don't know what to feed it.

- I had amnesia once...or twice.

- I went to San Francisco. I found someone's heart. Now what?

- Protons have mass? I didn't even know they were Catholic.

- All I ask is a chance to prove that money can't make me happy.

- If the world were a logical place, men would ride horses sidesaddle.

- What is a 'free' gift? Aren't all gifts free?
- They told me I was gullible...and I believed them.
- Teach a child to be polite and courteous in the home, and when he grows up, he'll never be able to merge his car onto a freeway.
- Two can live as cheaply as one, for half as long.
- The cost of living hasn't affected its popularity.
- How can there be self-help 'groups'?
- The speed of time is one-second per second.
- Is it possible to be totally partial?
- What's another word for thesaurus?
- Is Marx's tomb a communist plot?
- If swimming is so good for your figure, how do you explain whales?
- Show me a man with both feet firmly on the ground, and I'll show you a man who can't get his pants off.
- It's not an optical illusion. It just looks like one.
- Is it my imagination, or do buffalo wings taste like chicken?
- When the only tool you own is a hammer, every problem begins to look like a nail.
- What was the greatest thing before sliced bread? Hmmm?
- My weight is perfect for my height – which varies.

LATEST INVESTMENT & RETIREMENT PLANNING ADVICE

If you had purchased $1,000 of Nortel stock one year ago, it would now be worth $49.00. With Enron, you would have had $16.50 left of the original $1,000. With WorldCom, you would have had less than $5 left. If you had purchased $1,000 of Delta Air Lines stock you would have $49 left.

But, if you had purchased $1,000 worth of beer/wine one year ago, drank all the beer/wine, then turned in the cans/bottles for the aluminum recycling refund, you would have had $214.00

Based on the above, the best current investment advice is to drink heavily and recycle.

RAMBLINGS OF A RETIRED MIND

I was thinking about how a status symbol of today is those cell phones that everyone has clipped onto their belt or purse. I can't afford one, so I'm wearing my garage door opener.

I also made a cover for my hearing aid and now I have what they call blue teeth, I think.

You know, I spent a fortune on deodorant before I realized that people didn't like me anyway.

I was thinking that women should put pictures of missing husbands on beer cans!

I was thinking about old age and decided that old age is 'when you still have something on the ball, but you are just too tired to bounce it.'

I thought about making a fitness movie for folks my age and call it 'Pumping Rust'.

I've gotten that dreaded furniture disease. That's when your chest is falling into your drawers!

When people see a cat's litter box they always say, 'Oh, have you got a cat?' Just once I'd like to say, 'No, it's for company!'

Employment application blanks always ask who is to be notified in case of an emergency. I think you should write, 'A Good Doctor'!

I was thinking about how people seem to read the Bible a whole lot more as they get older. Then, it dawned on me. They were cramming for their finals.

Birds of a feather flock together....and then poop on your car.

A penny saved is a government oversight.

The older you get, the tougher it is to lose weight, because by then your body and your fat have gotten to be really good friends.

Quips, Quotes, Zingers & One Liners

The easiest way to find something lost around the house is to buy a replacement.

He who hesitates is probably right.

Did you ever notice: The Roman Numerals for forty are XL.

If you can smile when things go wrong, you have someone in mind to blame.

The sole purpose of a child's middle name is so he can tell when he's really in trouble.

Did you ever notice that when you put the 2 words, 'The' and 'IRS' together it spells 'Theirs'?

Eventually you will reach a point when you stop lying about your age and start bragging about it.

Some people try to turn back their odometers. Not me, I want people to know 'why' I look this way. I've traveled a long way and some of the roads weren't paved.

When you are dissatisfied and would like to go back to your youth, think of Algebra.

You know you are getting old when everything either dries up or leaks.

One of the many things no one tells you about aging is that it is such a nice change.

Being young is beautiful, but being old is comfortable.

SELF DEPRECIATION

We are what we eat,
which makes me fast and cheap.

My greatest fear is that there is no PMS and this is my real personality.

I DON'T SUFFER FROM INSANITY;
I ENJOY EVERY MINUTE OF IT.

Out of my mind. Back in five minutes.

You're just jealous because the voices only talk to me.

**Sometimes I pretend to be NORMAL, but it gets boring…
*so I go back to being me.***

Out for lunch,
If not back by five
Out for dinner as well.

I'M NOT GOOFING OFF,
I'M PACING MYSELF.

I'm just a Raggedy Ann in a Barbie Doll world.

I live in my own little world, but it's okay, they know me here.

YOU CAN'T STAY YOUNG FOREVER, BUT YOU CAN BE IMMATURE FOR THE REST OF YOUR LIFE.

SEX

My girlfriend always laughs during sex – no matter what she's reading.
Steve Jobs

Clinton lied. A man might forget where he parks or where he lives, but he never forgets oral sex, no matter how bad it is.
Barbara Bush

~~~

NOW THAT FOOD HAS REPLACED SEX IN MY LIFE,
I CAN'T EVEN GET INTO MY OWN PANTS.

If it works, call everyone you know with the good news!!

SEX AT 83!

I just took a leaflet out of my mailbox, informing me that I can have sex at 83!

I'm sooooo happy, because I live at unit 81....so it's not far to walk home afterwards!

~~~

After the eighty-three-year-old lady finished her annual physical examination, the doctor said, "You are in fine shape for your age, but tell me, do you still have intercourse?"

"Just a minute, I'll have to ask my husband," she said.

She stepped out into the crowded reception room and yelled out loud, "Henry, do we still have intercourse?"

You could hear a pin drop, there was a hush....

He answered impatiently, "If I told you once, Maxine, I told you a hundred times...what we have is Blue Cross!"

SIGNS

On a maternity room door:
Push. Push. Push.

At an optometrist's office:
If you don't see what you're looking for, you've come to the right place.

On a taxidermist's window:
We really know our stuff.

In a podiatrist's office:
Time wounds all heels.

On a fence:
Salesmen welcome! Dog food is expensive.

On a septic tank truck:
We're #1 in the #2 business.

At a gynecologist's office:
Dr. Jones, at your cervix

At a proctologist's office:
To expedite your visit please back in.

On a plumber's truck:
We repair what your husband fixed

Pizza shop slogan:
7 days without pizza makes one weak

At a tire shop:
Invite us to your next blowout.

At a plastic surgeon's office
Hello, can we pick your nose?

At a car dealership:
The best way to get back on your feet – miss a car payment.

Outside a muffler shop:
No appointment necessary. We hear you coming.

In a veterinarian's office:
Be back in 5 minutes. Sit! Stay!

At the electric company:
We would be delighted if you send in your payment. However, if you don't, you will be.

In a restaurant window:
Don't stand there and be hungry. Come on in and get fed up.

A funeral home parking lot:
Drive carefully. We'll wait.

At a propane filling station:
Tank heaven for little grills.

A radiator shop:
Best place in town to take a leak.

At a restaurant:
All drinking water in this establishment has been personally passed by the manager.

At a driving school:
If your wife wants to learn to drive, don't stand in her way.

Please don't throw your cigarette ends on the floor, the cockroaches are getting cancer.

Caution:
This Machine Has No Brain, Use Your Own

Sign in a bar:
Those of you who are drinking to forget, please do pay in advance.

Sign at barber's saloon:
We need your heads to run our business.

Written on a restaurant table:
We waited 30 minutes – no service!

Sporting goods store window:
Now is the winter of our discount tents.

Caution:
Truck may be transporting political promises.

On a septic truck:
Caution: Stool Bus

On a beauty parlor window:
Don't whistle at the girls going out from here. She may be your grandmother!

Visitors:
It's not always this messy here. Sometimes it's worse!

On a septic truck:
Yesterday's Meals on Wheels

In a hospital waiting room:
Smoking helps you lose weight…one lung at a time.

On a bulletin board:
Success is relative. The more success, the more the relatives.

Retail store front window:
Mr. Toskana has had an expensive divorce and now needs the money, so SALE NOW ON!!

At a zoo:
Please be safe.
Do not stand, sit, climb or lean on
zoo fences. If you fall, animals
could eat you and that might make
them sick. Thank you!

In a Bangkok temple:
It is forbidden to enter a woman, even
a foreigner, if dressed as a man.

Tokyo hotel rules and regulations:
Guests are requested not to
smoke, or do other disgusting
behaviours in bed.

Ad for donkey rides in Thailand:
Would you like to ride on your own
ass?

In a cemetary:
Persons are prohibited from
picking flowers from any but their
own graves.

On a poster:
Are you an adult that cannot read?
If so, we can help.

In an Abu Dhabi shop window:
If the front is closed, please enter
through my backside.

A sign in Germany's Black Forest:
It is strictly forbidden on our Black
Forest camping site that people of
different sex, for instance, men and
women, live together in one tent,
unless they are married with each
other for this purpose.

On the road to Mombasa, leaving
Nairobi:
Take notice – when this sign is
under water, this road is
impassable.

On a Swiss Restaurant menu:
Our wines leave you nothing to
hope for.

A laundry in Rome:
Ladies, leave your clothes here
and then spend the afternoon
having a good time.

In a Nairobi restaurant:
Customers who find our waitresses
rude, ought to see the manager.

At a hotel in Japan:
You are invited to take advantage
of the chambermaid.

Cocktail lounge in Norway:
Ladies are requested not to have
children in the bar.

At a hotel in Zurich:
Because of the impropriety of
entertaining guests of the opposite
sex in the bedroom, it is suggested
that the lobby be used for this
purpose.

Moscow hotel lobby, across from
Russian Orthodox Monestery:
You are welcome to visit the
cemetary where famous Russian
and Soviet composers, artists and
writers are buried daily, except
Thursday

Quips, Quotes, Zingers & One Liners

Airline ticket office:
We take your bags and send them
in all directions (Just like British
Airways)

A drycleaners in Bangkok:
Drop your trousers here for the
best results.

At a doctor's office in Rome:
Specialist in women and other
diseases

At a bar in Toyko:
Special cocktails for the ladies with
nuts.

At a city restaurant:
Open Seven Days A Week and
Weekends

SO WHAT ELSE IS NEW

Quips, Quotes, Zingers & One Liners

IDIOT SIGHTINGS

I handed the teller at my bank a withdrawal slip for $400.00 and I said, "May I have large bills, please?" She looked at me and said, "I'm sorry sir, all the bills are the same size." When I got up off the floor I explained it to her...

When my husband and I arrived at an automobile dealership to pick up our car, we were told the keys had been locked in it. We went to the service department and found a mechanic working feverishly to unlock the driver side door. As I watched from the passenger side, I instinctively tried the door handle and discovered that it was unlocked, "Hey," I announced to the technician, "it's open!" His reply, "I know, I already got that side."

We had to have the garage door repaired. The Sears repairman told us that one of our problems was that we did not have a 'large' enough motor on the opener. I thought for a minute, and said that we had the largest one Sears made at that time, a ½ horsepower. He shook his head and said, "Lady, you need a ¼ horsepower." I responded that ½ was larger than ¼. He said, "No, it's not. Four is larger than two."

My daughter and I went through the McDonald's take-out window and I gave the clerk a $5 bill. Our total was $4.25, so I also handed her a quarter. She said, "You gave me too much money." I said, "Yes I know, but this way you can just give me a dollar bill back." She sighed and went to get the manager, who asked me to repeat my request. I did so and he handed me back the quarter, and said, "We're sorry but we could not do that kind of thing." The clerk then proceeded to give me back $1 and 75 cents in change.

I live in a semi-rural area. We recently had a new neighbor call the local township administrative office to request the removal of the DEER CROSSING sign on our road. The reason, "Too many deer are being hit by cars out here! I don't think this is a good place for them to be crossing anymore."

My daughter went to a local Taco Bell and ordered a taco. She asked the person behind the counter for 'minimal lettuce.' He said he was sorry, but they only had iceburg lettuce.

I was at the airport, checking in at the gate when an airport employee asked, "Has anyone put anythng in your baggage without your knowledge?" To which I replied, "If it was without my knowledge, how would I know?" He smiled knowingly and nodded, "That's why we ask."

The stoplight on the corner buzzes when it's safe to cross the street. I was crossing with an intellectually challenged coworker of mine. She asked if I knew what the buzzer was for. I explained that it signals blind people when the light is red. Appalled, she responded, "What on earth are blind people doing driving?"

At a goodbye luncheon for an old and dear coworker who was leaving the company due to 'downsizing', our manager commented cheerfully, "This is fun. We should do this more often." Not another word was spoken. We all just looked at each other with that deer-in-the-headlights stare.

I work with an individual who plugged her power strip back into itself and for the sake of her life, couldn't understand why her system would not turn on.

How would you pronounce this child's name?
"Le-a"
Leah? No
Lee-A? No
Lay-a? No
Lei? Guess again.
This child attends a school in Kansas City. Her mother is irate because everyone is getting her name wrong. It's pronounced "Ledasha". When the mother was asked about the pronunciation of the name, she said, "the dash don't be silent."

SPORTS

Golf can be defined as an endless series of tragedies obscured by the occasional miracle, followed by a good bottle of beer. Golf! You hit down to make the ball go up. You swing left and the ball goes right. The lowest score wins. And on top of that, the winner buys the drinks. Golf is harder than baseball. In golf, you have to play your foul balls. If you find you do not mind playing golf in the rain, the snow, even during a hurricane, here's a valuable tip: your life is in trouble.

Golfers who try to make everything perfect before taking the shot rarely make a perfect shot. The term 'mulligan' is really a contraction of the phrase 'maul it again.'

A 'gimme' can best be defined as an agreement between two golfers...neither of whom can putt very well.

An interesting thing about golf is that no matter how badly you play, it is always possible to get worse. Golf's a hard game to figure out. One day you'll go out and slice it and shank it, hit into all the traps and miss every green. The next day you go out and for no reason at all you really stink.

If your best shots are the practice swing and the 'gimme putt', you might wish to reconsider this game. Golf is the only sport where the most feared opponent is you.

Golf is like marriage: if you take yourself too seriously, it won't work, and both are expensive. The best wood in most amateurs' bags is the pencil.

David Letterman's Top Ten Reasons Why Golf Is Better Than Sex

10) A below par performance is considered damn good.

9) You can stop in the middle and have a cheeseburger and a couple of beers.

8) It's much easier to find the sweet spot.

7) Foursomes are encouraged.

6) You can still make money doing it as a senior.

5) Three times a day is possible.

4) Your partner doesn't hire a lawyer if you play with someone else.

3) If you live in Florida, you can do it almost every day.

2) You don't have to cuddle with your partner when you're finished.

And the number one reason why golf is better than sex....

1) When your equipment gets old you can replace it!

Actual Calls Received At The Public Golf Course

Staff: Golf course, may I help you?
Caller: What are your green fees?
Staff: 38 dollars.
Caller: Does that include golf?

Staff: Golf course, may I help you?
Caller: Yes, I need to get some information from you. First, is this your correct phone number?

Staff: Golf course, may I help you?
Caller: Yes, we have a tee time for two weeks from Friday. What's the weather going to be like that day?

Staff: Golf course, may I help you?
Caller: Yes, I had a tee time for this afternoon but I'm running late. Can you still get me out early?

Staff: Golf course, may I help you?
Caller: Yes, do you have one of those areas where you can buy a bucket of golf balls and hit them for practice?
Staff: You mean a driving range?
Caller: No, that's not it.

Staff: Golf course, may I help you?
Caller: Yes, I'd like to get a tee time tomorrow between 12 o'clock and noon.
Staff: Between 12 o'clock and noon?
Caller: Yes.
Staff: We'll try to squeeze you in.

Staff: Golf course, may I help you?
Caller: Do you have any open tee times around 10 o'clock?
Staff: Yes, we have one at 10:15.
Caller: What's the next time after that?
Staff: We have one at 10:22.
Caller: We'll take that one. It will be a bit warmer.

Staff: Golf course, may I help you?
Caller: How much to play golf today?
Staff: 25 to walk, 38 with a cart.
Caller: 38 dollars?
Staff: No, 38 yen.

Staff: Golf course, may I help you?
Caller: What do you have for tee times tomorrow?
Staff: What time would you like?
Caller: What times do you have?
Staff: What time of the day?
Caller: Any time.
Staff: Morning or afternoon?
Caller: Whenever.
Staff: We have 16 times open in the morning and 20 open in the afternoon. Would you like me to read the whole list?
Caller: No, I don't think any of those times will work for me.

Staff: Golf course, may I help you?
Caller: Do you have a dress code?
Staff: Yes, we do. We require soft spikes.
Caller: How about clothes?
Staff: Yes, you have to wear clothes.

Staff: Golf course, may I help you?
Caller: Yes, do you have a driving range there?
Staff: Yes.
Caller: How much for a bucket of large balls?
Staff: Sorry, we're all out of large balls. But we can give you twice as many small balls for the same price.

Staff: Golf course, may I help you?
Caller: Can I get a tee time for tomorrow?
Staff: Sure, what time would you like?
Caller: Something between 9 o'clock and 10 o'clock. In the morning, if possible.

Staff: Golf course, may I help you?
Caller: Do you rent golf clubs there?
Staff: Yes, they're 25 dollars.
Caller: How much to rent a bag?

Staff: Golf course, may I help you?
Caller: Yes, my husband just called me on his cell phone and told me he's on the 15th hole. How many more holes does he have to play before he gets to the 18th?

Staff: Golf course, may I help you?
Caller: Yes, do you have a driving range there?
Staff: Yes.
Caller: How much for a large bucket?
Staff: Four dollars.
Caller: Does that include the balls?

Staff: Golf course, may I help you?
Caller: Do you have a twilight rate?
Staff: Yes, it's 15 dollars after 2 o'clock.
Caller: And what time does that start?

Staff: Golf course, may I help you?
Caller: Yes, I'd like some info about your golf course.
Staff: OK, what would you like to know?
Caller: I don't know, that's why I called.

Staff: Golf course, may I help you?

Caller: My kids just came home with pockets full of range balls and said they stole them from your driving range. Would you like to buy them back?

~~~

The way I putted,I must have been reading the greens in Spanish and putting them in English.
Homero Blancas

A game in which one endeavors to control a ball with implements ill adapted for the purposes.
U.S. President Woodrow Wilson

Don Quixote would understand golf. It is the impossible dream.
Legendary Sportswriter Jim Murray

I have a tip that can take five strokes off anyone's golf game; it's called an eraser.
Arnold Palmer

Golf balls are attracted to water as unerringly as the eye of a middle-aged man to a female bosom.
Writer Michael Green

I'm hitting the woods just great...but I'm having a terrible time getting them out.
Harry Toscano

If God wants to produce the ideal golfer then He should create a being with a set of unequal arms and likewise legs, an elbow-free left arm, knees which hinge sideways and a ribless torso from which emerges, at an angle of 45 degrees, a stretched neck fitted with one color-blind eye stuck firmly on the left side.
Golf Writer Chris Plumridge

What goes up must come down. But don't expect it to come down where you can find it.
Comedian Lily Tomlin

I always said you have to be really smart or really dumb to play this game well. I just don't know where I fit in.
Beth Daniel

Quips, Quotes, Zingers & One Liners

Golf is a game that is played on a five-inch course – the distance between your ears.
Golf Legend Bobby Jones

The worst club in my bag is my brain.
Chris Perry

I'f I'm on the course and lightning starts, I get inside fast. If God wants to play through, let him.
Bob Hope

The real reason your pro tells you to keep your head down is so you can't see him laughing at you.
Phyllis Diller

His driving is unbelievable. I don't go that far on my holidays
Ian Baker Finch

One of the advantages bowling has over golf is that you seldom lose a bowling ball.
Bowling Legend Don Carter

I don't say my golf game is bad, but if I grew tomatoes, they'd come up sliced.
Miller Barber

My swing is so bad I look like a caveman killing his lunch
Lee Trevino

It's so bad I could putt off a tabletop and still leave the ball halfway down the leg.
J.C. Snead

No golfer can ever become too good to practice.
Legendary British Ladies Champion May Hezley

Don't be too proud to take lessons. I'm not.
Jack Nicklaus

Second doesn't matter. Second is about as important as fifty-second. Winning is the reason you're playing.
Arnold Palmer

Nobody ever remembers who finished second at anything.
Jack Nicklaus

When you finish second, you are at the front of a long line of losers.
Anonymous

Someone once told me that there is more to life than golf. I think it was my ex-wife.
Bruce Lansky

Golf is a game in which you yell 'Fore', shoot six and write down five.
Broadcaster Paul Harvey

You can talk to a fade but a hook won't listen.
Lee Trevino

There are two things you can do with your head down – play golf and pray.
Lee Trevino

Prayer never works for me on the golf course. That may have something to do with my being a terrible putter.
Reverend Billy Graham

One day I did get angry with myself and threw a club. My caddy told me, "You're not good enough to get mad."
Actor Samuel L. Jackson

My game is so bad I gotta hire three caddies: one to walk the left rough, one for the right rough, and one down the middle. And the one in the middle doesn't have much to do.
Dave Hill

ANYONE CAN PLAY GOLF

Once a player has mastered the grip and stance, all he has to bear in mind, in the brief two-second interval it takes to swing, is to keep his left elbow pointed in toward the left hip and his right arm loose and closer to the body than the left and take the club head past his right knee and then break the wrists at just the right instant while the left arm is still traveling straight back from the ball and the right arm stays glued to the body and the hips come around in a perfect circle and meanwhile everything is mucked up unless the weight is 60 percent on the left foot and 40 percent on the right not an ounce more or less and at just the right point in the turn the left knee bends in toward the right in a dragging motion until the left heel comes off the ground but not too far and be sure the hands are over the right foot but not on the toe more than the heel except that the left side of the right foot is tilted off the ground but not too far and be sure the hands at the top of the swing are high and the shaft points along a line parallel with the ground and if its a downhill lie the shaft is supposed to be pointed downhill too and pause at the top of the swing and count one, jerk the left arm straight down like a bell ringer yanking a belfry rope and don't uncock the wrists too soon and pull the left hip around in a circle but don't let the shoulders turn with the hips, they have to be facing the hole and now transfer the weight 60 percent to the left foot and 40 percent to the right not an ounce more or less and tilt the left foot now so the right side of it is straight that's the one you hit against watch out for the left hand, it's supposed to be extended but not too stiff or the shot won't go anywhere and don't let it get loose or you will hook and let the wrists uncock but don't force them or you'll smother the shot and don't break too soon but keep your head down then hit the ball! THAT'S ALL THERE IS TO IT.

ADDITIONS TO THE SANTA ROSA GOLF MANUAL

1) How to properly line up your fourth putt.

2) How to hit a Nike from the rough after you'd hit a Titleist from the tee.

3) How to avoid the water when you lie 8 in the bucking funker.

4) How to get more distance from the shank.

5) Proper excuses for drinking beer before 9 a.m.

6) How to find that ball that everyone else saw go into the water.

7) Why your spouse couldn't care less that you birdied the thirteenth.

8) How to let a foursome play through your twosome.

9) When to suggest Major Swing Corrections to your opponent.

10) How to relax when you're hitting three off the tee.

11) When to re-grip your ball retriever, and..

Quips, Quotes, Zingers & One Liners
348

12) Why male golfers will happily pay $5.00 for a beer from the cute golf cart girl and give her a $3.00 tip, but will bitch about a $3.50 beer at the 19th hole and stiff the bartender.

THE TWELVE GOLFING DAYS OF CHRISTMAS

On the first day of Christmas, my true love sent to me, a double bogey on a par three.

On the second day of Christmas, my true love sent to me, two total whiffs, and a double bogey on a par three.

On the third day of Christmas, my true love sent to me, three lost balls, two total whiffs, and a double bogey on a par three.

On the fourth day of Christmas, my true love sent to me, four curving putts, three lost balls, two total whiffs, and a double bogey on a par three.

On the fifth day of Christmas, my true love sent to me, five broken tees, four curving putts, three lost balls, two total whiffs, and a double bogey on a par three.

On the sixth day of Christmas, my true love sent to me, six rotten lies, five broken tees, four curving putts, three lost balls, two total whiffs, and a double bogey on a par three.

On the seventh day of Christmas, my true love sent to me, seven lakes a-waiting, six rotten lies, five broken tees, four curving putts, three lost balls, two total whiffs, and a double bogey on a par three.

On the eighth day of Christmas, my true love sent to me, eight bunkers bunking, seven lakes a-waiting, six rotten lies, five broken tees, four curving putts, three lost balls, two total whiffs, and a double bogey on a par three.

On the ninth day of Christmas, my true love sent to me, nine creeks a-creeking, eight bunkers bunking, seven lakes a-waiting, six rotten lies, five broken tees, four curving putts, three lost balls, two total whiffs, and a double bogey on a par three.

On the tenth day of Christmas, my true love sent to me, ten geese a-crapping, nine creeks a-creeking, eight bunkers bunking, seven lakes a-waiting, six rotten lies, five broken tees, four curving putts, three lost balls, two total whiffs, and a double bogey on a par three.

On the eleventh day of Christmas, my true love sent to me, eleven shots a-dribbling, ten geese a-crapping, nine creeks a-creeking, eight bunkers bunking, seven lakes a-waiting, six rotten lies, five broken tees, four curving putts, three lost balls, two total whiffs, and a double bogey on a par three.

On the the twelfth day of Christmas, my true love sent to me, twelve wicked slices, eleven shots a-dribbling, ten geese a-crapping, nine creeks a-creeking, eight bunkers bunking, seven lakes a-waiting, six rotten lies, five broken tees, four curving putts, three lost balls, two total whiffs, and a double bogey on a par three.

By Bruce Elder

WORDS

```
┌─────────────────────────────────────────┐
│          Word Of The Day:                │
│             EXHAUSTED                     │
│     Just too tired to give a shit!       │
└─────────────────────────────────────────┘
```

THIS WEIRD ENGLISH

We'll begin with a box, and the plural is boxes,
But the plural of ox becomes oxen, not oxes.
One fowl is a goose, but two are called geese,
Yet the plural of moose should never be meese.
You may find a lone mouse or a nest full of mice,
Yet the plural of house is houses, not hice.

If the plural of man is always called men,
Why shouldn't the plural of pan be called pen?
If I speak of my foot and show you my feet,
And I give you a boot, would a pair be called beet?
If one is a tooth and a whole set are teeth,
Why shouldn't the plural of booth be called beeth?

If the singular is this and the plural is these,
Should the plural of kiss not therefore be kese?
Then one may be that, and three may be those.
Yet, the plural of hat would never be hose.

We speak of a brother and brethren,
But though we say mother, we never say methren.
The masculine pronouns are he, his or him,
But imagine the feminine, she, shis or shim!

So our English I think you all will agree is the weirdest language you ever
did see.

~~~

Think: What you do when you can't thwim?

Quips, Quotes, Zingers & One Liners
353

Made in the USA
Columbia, SC
23 April 2021